# The Miracle of Prayer

## TRUE STORIES OF BLESSED HEALINGS

Here are the stories of . . . Ann Marie Davis, who, through her own prayers and those of family, friends, and prayer circles, overcame four recurrences of cancer, confounding doctors who at one point had given her only three hours to live. . . . Maurice Williams, who survived two kidney transplants and conceived his "Five Steps to Systematic Healing," the first of which is forgiveness. . . . Joan, who lost her faith when her house burned down, but began to pray again when faced with cancer surgery. She was wheelchair-bound until a visit from an angel filled her room with light and enabled her to walk unaided. . . . John, whose frightened prayers for his radiologist to be guided during a tricky angiogram were answered. As the doctor removed his mask after successfully completing the procedure, John saw the face of an angel superimposed over the doctor's own. . . .

**Also by Rosemary Ellen Guiley**

*Tales of Reincarnation*

*Angels of Mercy*

# THE Miracle OF Prayer

## True Stories of Blessed Healings

## ROSEMARY ELLEN GUILEY

POCKET BOOKS

New York   London   Toronto   Sydney   Tokyo   Singapore

An *Original* Publication of POCKET BOOKS

POCKET BOOKS, a division of Simon & Schuster Inc.
1230 Avenue of the Americas, New York, NY 10020

Guiley, Rosemary,
    The miracle of prayer : true stories of blessed healings / Rosemary Ellen Guiley.
      p.  cm.
    ISBN 0-671-75692-3
    1. Healing—Religious aspects—Case studies.  2. Prayer—Case studies.  I. Title.
    BL65.M5G85   1995
    242'.4—dc20                      95-5082
                                                  CIP

First Pocket Books trade paperback printing April 1995

10   9   8   7   6   5   4   3   2   1

POCKET and colophon are registered trademarks of Simon & Schuster Inc.

Cover design by Joanna Reisman
Front cover illustration reproduced courtesy of the
   Trustees, The National Gallery, London
Text design by Stanley S. Drate/Folio Graphics Co. Inc.

Printed in the U.S.A.

Excerpts from the Bible taken from the Revised Standard Version (Zondervan Bible Publishers, 1946, 1952, 1970; Grand Rapids, Michigan).

For Tom Wright

*fide et amor*

# ACKNOWLEDGMENTS

I am deeply indebted to the persons whose prayer stories appear in the book: Sue,* Joan,* Guy Riggs, Ann Marie Davis, Maurice Williams, Jim Rosemergy, Chris Jackson, Kai Kermani, M.D., Father John Murray, Diadra, Boyce Batey, and John. I am also indebted to others who gave me interviews and material: Daniel J. Benor, M.D., Spindrift, Inc., Rev. Richard L. Batzler, Rev. Lawrence W. Althouse, and the Johrei Fellowship. A very special thanks goes to Richard and Mary-Alice Jafolla, codirectors of Silent Unity, who opened their doors and their hearts to me; to Carol Riead, director of public relations at the Unity School of Christianity, who went the distance to help me find what I needed for the book; and to all the persons at Unity who shared their experiences (some of whom must remain anonymous because of their work with prayer). I am also grateful to Elizabeth W. Fenske, executive director of the Spiritual Frontiers Fellowship International, and to Boyce Batey, executive secretary of the Academy of Religion and Psychical Research, both of whom made it possible for me to meet some of the persons featured in this book. Thanks also to Rhea A. White, founder of Psi Information Resource Center, and to Joanne McMahon, librarian of the Parapsychology Foundation, for their assistance. And finally, I am especially grateful to Tom Wright, whose love and support made this work possible.

*These names have been changed to protect the identities of the individuals involved.

# CONTENTS

## Chapter One
### "THEY WERE SURE I WAS GOING TO DIE"

*Doctors said there was no hope, but prayer and determination bring a woman suffering from cancer and Legionnaires' disease back from the brink of death.*

## Chapter Two
### THE ESSENCE OF PRAYER

*Prayer is difficult to define, but our attempts to do so give us insight into its mysterious powers.*

## Chapter Three
### "WOULD MY NEXT MOVE BE MY LAST?"

*A young man lies stranded with a fractured back on a deserted rocky beach, with nothing but prayer, positive thought, and hope to help him hold on.*

# Chapter Four

## PRAYER, PSI, AND HEALING

*Prayer is closely associated with psi, and both are crucial in healing.*

# Chapter Five

## PRAYER AND THE POWER OF THOUGHT

*All of our thoughts are prayers, and thought creates reality—so discover a husband and wife who heal themselves of a shriveled leg, partial deafness, and tuberculosis.*

# Chapter Six

## "EVERYONE IS CAPABLE OF A MIRACLE"

*A doctor uses prayer and relaxation to heal himself of blindness—twice—and becomes a spiritual healer, whose patients include AIDS sufferers.*

# Chapter Seven

## THE ART OF SUCCESSFUL PRAYER

*Healers, clergy, doctors, scientists, and mystics discuss how to maximize the effectiveness of prayer.*

# INTRODUCTION

The purpose of this book is to expand our horizons on prayer: what it is, how it works, and why it is important to our collective spiritual evolution. Prayer is a tangible force; it has tangible power. Prayer is perhaps most dramatic in its power when it is an instrument for healing. In these pages, you will hear from many men and women, from all walks of life and facing all kinds of situations, who experienced the miraculous in healing when they turned to prayer.

I've had my own witnessing to the power of prayer in healing. In the mid-1980s, I began to suffer frequent and severe abdominal pain, and consulted my doctor. My diagnosis was an ovarian cyst. Ultrasound examination revealed it to be of considerable size: 4 cm × 3 cm × 3.1 cm. It was recommended that I monitor it with annual ultrasound, and that if it began increasing in size, I should have it surgically removed without delay.

The cyst remained the same size for several years, and the pain associated with it was intermittent. At the time, I believed—as I still do today—that the occurrence of the cyst was related to emotional blockages and anger having to do with my personal life. I worked on resolving those issues.

When I had accomplished a resolution, I began work on the cyst with visualization, prayer, and energy-transfer healing. In September 1993, the cyst was still present, and once again I was urged to consider surgery. Though I still wished to avoid surgery, I did begin to contemplate that avenue. I continued with prayer and visualization, and had two more energy-transfer healings, one in the United States and one in England. In July 1994, I had a routine pelvic examination, and it was discovered that my cyst had disappeared. The doctor's only explanation was, "These things happen."

Indeed they do. They happen when we align to the power of God, to the life force of the universe.

Some years ago, I did research on prayer for another project. I was astonished at the literature on experiments with prayer using plants, organisms, healers, and human subjects. It by no means rivaled the research of even psi, let alone other subjects, but it was far more than I had expected to find. Yet prayer seemed to be in a backwater, stuck in church and in the hospital. Prayer, I thought, deserves a better place on our list of priorities in life.

In 1993, a book was published that did much to bring prayer back into a spotlight. Larry Dossey, M.D., well-known for his inquiries into alternative healing and spirituality, wrote *Healing Words,* an engrossing work on prayer and medicine. It is my hope that this book, *The Miracle of Prayer: True Stories of Blessed Healings,* will add to the interest and insight, and inspire people to prayer.

The scope of this book focuses on healing and on our spiritual evolution, in which prayer plays an important role. The emphasis here is on direct experience, which demonstrates the mystery and power of prayer. The book also covers science, healing, metaphysics, and mysticism.

I have not delved into denominations and faiths. Every religion, every denomination, has its own approach to prayer. While religion can acquaint us with prayer and further our understanding of it, it can also restrict our view of it. To fully appreciate and use the awesome power of prayer, we must be as open and as flexible as possible in our approach to it. As many of the people in these pages testify, their conventional, religious views on prayer were stretched by their experiences. With this in mind, I have gone to nondenominational approaches to prayer, such as Unity and Science of Mind, movements which espouse principles applicable to all faiths.

During my research on this book, I had occasion to discuss prayer with a friend and colleague, Boyce Batey, of Bloomfield, Connecticut. Boyce is executive secretary of the Academy of Religious and Psychical Research, an academic affiliate of the Spiritual Frontiers Fellowship International.

Boyce is a longtime student of metaphysical and mystical pursuits. His spiritual path is largely the result of a profound mystical experience he had in 1954 at age twenty-one. While relaxed and enjoying a poem by William Wordsworth, *The Prelude,* Boyce decided to try an experiment to achieve total awareness of all his senses simultaneously. He concentrated on one sense at a time, adding them together so that he could experience them all at the same time.

He was flooded with sensations and then suddenly became aware that his consciousness was functioning on another level of awareness or dimension. "A great white light surrounded me completely and was within me and outside of me, beating and pulsating with me and outside of me at the same time," he recounted. "I was that light, that light was me. That light was God and I was God. My being was within me and outside of me at the same time. Everything outside of me was within me and was me. Everything within me was outside of me and was me.

"There was no separation, there were no boundaries. I was one with all and all was one within me. There was in my being a sense of love, peace, joy, and exultation in dimensions and quality in consciousness that I have never before nor since experienced. There was no past or future; all time was now. It was as though I was aware of the laws of the universe and the meaning of existence. I knew that the drift of the cosmos ultimately was toward good, that there was only good and no evil in the universe, that there was no death, that all was Life and Life was God and God was Love and that I was God."

This experience lasted an estimated eight seconds, yet it was eternal in nature. It took Boyce several weeks to integrate it. His values changed as a result—his spiritual values went up, and his material interests went down. He had been a devout, church-going Episcopalian. After the experience, church rituals lost meaning, and he didn't much attend church. He was less religious, but far more spiritual. "I knew of a greater reality," he said. "Before the experience, I believed in God. After the experience, I no longer believed in God—I knew that God *is*. For me, it was the knowing of God firsthand."

Prayer is a vital part of Boyce's spiritual life, an essential exercise in his endeavors to attune with God. "Prayer means to be in communion with the highest level of consciousness in the universe, which in my experience is God," said Boyce. "Prayer is communing with the highest part of my own being and with the deepest guidance and wisdom of the universe. Prayer brings healing, especially if you know how to pray. For prayer to be effective, you have to be absolutely honest with yourself and with God."

Boyce shared with me an interesting experience he had during a shamanic journey he undertook under the guidance of a transpersonal psychologist in May 1994. In it, he received a message about the importance of prayer:

To the sound of drumming, I went down into a cleft in a large weeping willow tree in my backyard in order to get into the underworld. As I got into the underworld I was in an environment of very lush greenery, where purple flowers grew. There I saw my power animal, an eagle, and asked it what wisdom it could share with me.

It said, "All is light." I asked if there was more to share, and it said, *"Nada."* I then came back up through the cleft in the weeping willow tree.

On the second journey, I went back down again through that cleft and came out this time into an environment of banyan trees, where the roots were huge and dwarfed me. Sitting on the root of a banyan tree, once again, was my power animal. I asked it to take me to the Spirit of the World, and we began going very rapidly into the center of the earth. There I met the Spirit of the World. It was a pulsating white light form of energy in the shape of a butterfly that was larger than the earth itself.

I asked it what I could do in my everyday life to be of help to the world. The Spirit of the World responded, "Pray, go within. The best way to do is to be."

Indeed, the best way we can pray is to be; that is, to pray with our lives—make our every thought, word, and deed a striving to align ourselves with the Divine.

We're more than ready to grow in this direction. Collectively, we're compelled to search for spiritual nourishment, for support, for some sense that we truly are part of a grand cosmic scheme that has no beginning and no end, but is eternal and born out of unconditional love. Prayer can answer those needs. And in the process of growing spiritually, of recognizing our eternal essence and our cosmic selves, we are healed.

—Rosemary Ellen Guiley
Annapolis, 1994

# One

## "They Were Sure I Was Going to Die"

I do believe in the power of prayer."

These firm words were spoken by someone who knows and appreciates their truth firsthand: Ann Marie Davis, an ordained Unity minister.

When I met Ann Marie, she was working at the Unity School of Christianity near Kansas City, Missouri, having recently graduated from its ministerial school. She had just gotten remarried two months previously to another ministerial graduate, and she and her new husband were awaiting their first church assignment (subsequently, they were posted to Cedar Rapids, Iowa). It was hard to believe that this blonde, energetic woman of forty-five had ever been seriously ill, let alone returned from the brink of what doctors said was certain death. Yet Ann Marie had bested a decades-long fight with cancer and had experienced a miraculous recovery from Legionnaires' disease that had left doctors shaking their heads in amazement.

Prayer was the cornerstone of her miracle.

Ann Marie grew up on a farm in Lake City, Minnesota. "I first got Hodgkin's disease at age ten," she said, recounting her harrowing, life-threatening experiences. "Back then, doctors didn't know much about it, and it took them a long time to figure out that's what I had. My chief symptom was extreme fatigue. I was a real tomboy, always climbing trees and carrying on. For me to suddenly be very tired showed something was very wrong. But by the time I was diagnosed, I had lost a lot of weight. I couldn't even walk a straight line, I was so thin.

"I was given radiation treatments. I was so tired, I really didn't care whether I lived or not. I remember telling my mother not to cry if I died because I'd be happier in heaven, where I wouldn't be tired and I would be able to run. But I also stuffed away a lot of emotions. We weren't the type of people to talk about our feelings, so I went into denial. Everybody told me I wasn't going to die, but I had already read in the medical books that I would.

"Radiation was fairly new at that time, and they had to experiment with the dosage. They gave me a small dosage, and so the cancer kept reoccurring through all my school years. They'd give me more radiation, and it would go away for a while, then come back. In all, I've been in and out of remission four times.

"Because it kept going away, I guess I didn't have a lot of fear about it. I had enough faith—and I knew there was a heaven. I wasn't really afraid of death. Once you face death, you kind of overcome it, even as a child. In fact, it's probably easier as a child. Basically, I still wanted to live, and because the cancer kept going away, I really trusted that the radiation would cure the cancer."

"Was prayer a part of your family life?" I asked. "When you got sick, did your family pray for you?"

"Yes, very much," said Ann Marie. "We were Catholic, and my mother's great prayer was a rosary. That was her power—prayer. Whenever it seemed there was no hope, she always said the rosary. I still say the rosary once in a while. I grew up with that prayer. Also, our prayers were beseeching—'Please, God, help us.' My mother had great faith that there was a God out there who would say yes or no to different prayers. I believed in a heaven and a hell. I had faith that I would be in heaven when I died.

"The last time I had radiation was when I was in the seventh or eighth grade. I'm hazy on the dates, I was so young when all this happened. At that time, they gave me a superdose, thinking that would eradicate it, which it did for twelve years. I considered myself cured. I graduated from school, got married, and had children.

"But when I was ten years old, I made beseeching prayers to God in order to cope with the cancer. I made a deal with God, asking him to at least let me live to be thirty. I thought thirty was so old, who would want to live any longer than that anyway! Of course, you get what you pray for—so when I was twenty-nine and a half I had a fourth recurrence of cancer."

"Did you think about that deal with God as you approached age thirty?" I asked.

"No, I didn't," said Ann Marie. "I had completely forgotten about it. Now I'm fully aware of the power of the spoken word!

"After I got the fourth recurrence, I was very angry. I thought, 'Why me? Why does this always have to happen to *me*?' Yet I was determined to make it through the ordeal once again. This time, I had had so much radiation that people joked that I glowed in the dark. They couldn't give me any more radiation, so they decided to do chemotherapy.

"The first thing they did was exploratory surgery where they opened me up and checked the cancer to see where it was and how far it had spread. I had never had major surgery before, so I didn't realize when I woke up how much pain I would be in. I really got scared then. I had to face the fact that this time I might die. In the past, I had always tried to deny the fact of death and believe that I was going to live. But with all the pain, plus being depressed from surgery, I began to think that four times was pushing my luck, and this time I might die.

"One night in the hospital, I was all alone in the room around eleven P.M. My family had left. I began to feel like a child wanting her mother. My own mother wasn't able to be there, so I said a very simple prayer. I said, 'Jesus, can I borrow your mother for a while? I really need a mother right now.'

The room was suddenly *filled* with the greatest feeling of love and joy and peace. I didn't see anything or hear any voices. I was just filled with such joy that I knew everything was going to be all right. Whether you call it Mary, the Goddess, the Divine Mother, or simply that part of God that is love, joy, and peace—that's what I really felt. I still knew I might die, but that didn't matter. All that mattered was the wonderful presence that was there with me in the room. I still had the pain, but the pain didn't matter. I was no longer afraid. I almost started laughing out loud, I was feeling such joy. I finally was able to go to sleep.

"After that, they started the chemotherapy, and the peace just stayed with me. They started the chemotherapy the day before Christmas, and I went to midnight Mass thinking that this was my last Christmas. I was very much at peace about it. It was like even though I still knew I might die, the peace from my experience continued to stay with me.

"The chemotherapy had harsh side effects. After a few months on chemotherapy, my immune system was so worn down that I caught Legionnaires' disease. That's worse than pneumonia.

"I didn't know what it was at first. It came on extremely fast. I woke up in the middle of the night and couldn't breathe. I was inhaling and I was exhaling, but I wasn't getting any oxygen. I thought I had a cold, then I realized it was worse than a cold. I thought it was probably pneumonia, but it was late at night, and I didn't want to call the doctors until morning. But I got so bad that my husband at that time rushed me to the emergency room in an ambulance.

"They took me to a small, local hospital that could not afford expensive life-support systems. They said I was dying and that there was nothing they could do, and that I was even too weak to survive an ambulance trip to Rochester. My white count at that point was ten, which meant I virtually didn't have a white count at all. They said there was nothing they could do, and they were sure I was going to die.

"Well, the next morning I was still alive. A Mayo Clinic doctor who came to this hospital every Saturday took one look at me and agreed that I was dying, but said that I needed to get to a hospital in Rochester because there they could keep me more comfortable until I died.

"At that point, my prayers were to die. I told everyone who came into my room that I just wanted to die. It was such an effort just to breathe, and I was feeling so awful, there was no way I wanted to live."

"Were you unable to get in touch with the Mary presence that has so filled you with joy before?" I asked.

"The peace and the joy didn't relate to whether or not I would live," answered Ann Marie. "Those feelings came from being with that presence, and I knew I would be with it whether I lived or died. It transcended life. You know, maybe there was a part of me that always wanted to be there on the other side rather than here, and maybe that's why I've always gotten sick and tried to check out. I'm not afraid of death."

Ann Marie resumed her story. "They did get me to the hospital in Rochester, and the doctors there all agreed that I was going to die. Only one doctor there said I needed to go on a respirator. The other doctors didn't want to do that, because they knew I was going to die. However, because the one doctor insisted that I go on a respirator, they put me on one.

"I have little memory of the next two weeks. I was on a lot of morphine for the pain. Still, I was awake, I was alert, I wasn't brain-dead, I knew what was happening to me. I could communicate by nodding my head. Others later told me that every day for two weeks, whatever could go wrong with me did go wrong. Every organ malfunctioned except for my heart and my brain. Every day the doctors said, 'She's dying, it's only a matter of time.' They kept doing things each day to keep me alive. They had to fill me with fluid—something about fluid on the heart. When they fill you with fluid, you're like a balloon. My eyes were bulged out with red sacks under them. I had no hair from my chemotherapy—I really looked like a monster. People came into my room and did not recognize me at all. I had fever blisters all over my mouth and in my mouth, because I had no immune system to fight against anything. Everywhere there was skin, there was an IV sticking in me. I had a tube down my mouth for breathing and another down my nose for eating. The respirator was doing all my breathing.

"One night I began to bleed internally. I was too weak for surgery. They inserted a syringe in my stomach and pumped ice water into me to stop the bleeding. Meanwhile, my family was praying for a miracle that I would live. I also had thousands of other people praying for me: friends and relatives and people who told people who told people. I was on many prayer chains and lists in group prayer circles. People of all denominations had me on their prayer chains.

"On Holy Thursday, the doctors called all my family in and said, 'Tonight's the night. She's going to die. There's no more chance. She's got from three to forty-eight hours left.' At that point my lungs had become brittle. Lungs are like rubber, and when they become brittle they cannot go back to being elastic. The doctors said that if by some miracle I lived, I would never get off a respirator.

"Once my family saw my X rays, and realized that if I lived I would always be on a respirator, they surrendered me to God. They said, 'All right, whatever your will is, God.' They knew it would be better for me to die than to live that way.

"All my family felt this way except for my then-husband, Bert, who came in and gently chewed me out. He said, 'You have always practiced positive thinking and have always told me and everyone else to let go and let God be in control. It's about time you started practicing what you preach. There's nothing anyone can do. The doctors can't do any more. You've got to surrender this to God.'

"I couldn't speak because of the tubes, but I nodded my head that I would surrender this to God. Then I went to sleep. Something happened while I was asleep.

"The next morning was Good Friday. When the doctors came back in, they were amazed, because my condition had completely reversed. Everything was functioning normally. My lungs, which had been brittle, were now elastic. They said the X rays from Thursday to Friday were totally different, like night into day.

"Not only that, but when they checked on the cancer a week later, they discovered it had completely disappeared. I had only been on chemotherapy for two or three months, and I was supposed to be on it for a year.

"The doctors didn't know what to say. They just came in and looked at me silently and smiled, and I looked back at them and smiled. We all just sat and smiled. They said they had no medical explanation for what happened. One of my sisters said, 'We think a miracle has happened, what do you think?' They just said, 'Well, we can't explain it.' "

"Bert really refused to give in," I commented.

Ann Marie nodded. "He never accepted that I would die. He is a very intuitive man. The doctors were upset with him for not accepting what seemed to be my impending death—they knew he would have to deal with it sooner or later. In particular, one doctor would say to Bert every time he saw him, 'Now, you know she's going to die. You've got to start accepting this.' We joked with that doctor afterward—he felt sheepish that I didn't die.

"That's my story. I think the biggest miracle, though, wasn't in my physical healing but the change in me—the change in my consciousness. When I came out of this, I was intensely interested in studying spirituality. I read the bible, which I had never done before. I got into almost a Fundamentalist attitude, that you have to accept Jesus. But then I realized that the Fundamentalists were judging people—'I'm saved and you're not'—and I couldn't handle that. So I studied other religions, searching to find a faith that would embrace all people. The more I studied, the more I realized that we are all the same, and we all worship the same God. I finally found my home in Unity, which embraces all faiths.

"The change in my consciousness happened gradually. I had grown up sick all the time, so I had a mentality of being sick: I always said I couldn't do this or that because I was sick. I had a consciousness of cancer. After this experience, I no longer had a consciousness of cancer or being sick. Now I know there is nothing that I can't do, and that I don't have to be sick. That was the biggest healing."

"How have the last fifteen years been for your health?" I asked.

"I'm now healthier than I've ever been," answered Ann Marie. "I've had no recurrence of cancer for fifteen years. Of course, now I know that I don't ever need to get sick again, unless on some level I choose to. But I no longer *choose* to get sick.

"It was still a long process to get better. The recovery is really the beginning of the rest of the story. I was in the hospital in intensive care for over a month and was weak from being bedridden. I was like a baby—I had to learn things over again. I had to learn how to sit up by myself, how to hold my head up, and how to raise my arms and legs. Eventually, I could sit up and I could stand, and then I had to learn how to walk again by taking a few steps at a time.

"Another problem that became evident was an addiction to morphine. I was on a lot of morphine for over two weeks. To get me off the morphine they put me on tranquilizers, which, unknown to me, were just as addictive. I didn't know I was addicted to the pills by the time I went home, and I threw away the pills they'd given me. I immediately began to suffer severe panic attacks from the withdrawal.

"At one point I went to a doctor for help with these attacks, and he just put me on more drugs—antidepressants—and of course they made me feel out of it. I decided not to take any drugs at all, but to deal with my recovery through my own strength. To me that meant prayer.

"There I was, so afraid, I couldn't even go outside my house. So, I set goals for myself. Each day I would go outside a little further. I'd go outside and come back in, and then I'd go outside and walk halfway down the street. The next day I'd go around the block. One day I went to visit my sister, but at some point I got scared and had to go home. I was afraid to tell anybody what was going on, for fear they'd think I was going crazy. Nobody except my immediate family knew or understood what I was going through.

"The hardest part of healing for me was making it through the panic attacks. But, every day it got better and better. As I got physically stronger, the panic attacks became less and less—eventually just once a day, or twice a week, or once a month. Finally, a year later, they were pretty well gone."

"How did prayer help you with your recovery?" I said.

"Prayer helped to give me strength and determination," said Ann Marie. "The doctors kept chewing me out for being so determined—I always walked more than I should have and did more than I should have and pushed myself harder than I should have done. But that strength in me from prayer was pushing me on, perhaps enabling me to carry on when other people might have stopped.

"After every accomplishment I made, they said I couldn't go past that point. When I got off the respirator, they said I would probably have to carry oxygen with me the rest of my life, and I just refused to do that. Whenever someone came to visit me, I asked them to pray that I would not have to be on oxygen the rest of my life. Every step I took, I did more than the doctors said I could do. Prayer helped me know there was a higher power that could help me overcome whatever anyone said I couldn't do. Prayer gave me faith and the strength and the courage to go on."

"How long did it take you to fully recover?"

"It took me a month to be able to walk around. I'd get so tired from the smallest exertion, even eating—I would sleep for an hour after eating. Walking a little bit made me huff and puff. Within two to three months I was nearly back to normal physically, but emotionally it took about a year to recover.

"My immune system was so weakened that years later I was struck by the Epstein-Barr syndrome—Bert and I both had it. We were tired all the time. We went out to Nevada to a holistic clinic. After a week or two there, I came back feeling stronger and healthier than ever before. I had energy like I had never had before. Since then, I've been healthier than ever. I do cough once in a while—there are still scars on my lungs—but that's it.

"The only really noticeable thing that happened is I'm deaf in my left ear. They've never ascertained exactly what happened, except some medications can take away your hearing.

"I'm a different person now. I now know that I don't have to be sick, and that I can be whatever I want to be. I used to think that because I was sick all the time, there were things I could do and things I couldn't do, and I was kind of wimpy. I had victim consciousness. Now I have more of a mastership consciousness.

"I consider surrender to Spirit the greatest and only kind of prayer. I think the only reason we have problems is because we're in a state of resistance. And if we can be in a state of nonresistance or surrender, we would probably not have so many problems."

I asked Ann Marie how she prays now.

"There are days when I do beg, but I know through what I've learned in metaphysics that affirmative prayer is most effective," she said. "There's no one way to pray. But I pray more affirmative prayers now. I also pray to surrender. That's the main one. When difficulties come, and they still do, my first reaction is to panic, and then I immediately have to surrender. Every time I surrender, the problem is taken care of. I'm always amazed at how things are solved if I just surrender.

"Another way I pray is what we in Unity call sitting in silence, in which we let go of thought. You can also call it meditation."

"What is your advice to others about prayer?" I asked.

"Surrender and trust—that's the quickest way to heal. And don't have attachment to the outcome—know that you can accept whatever the outcome is. Sometimes there is healing in death. I would also advise sitting in the silence and experiencing God. I believe it was Leon Bloy who said that joy is the most infallible sign of the presence of God. I add to that, when you're feeling joy, you're feeling the kingdom of God. We should not be so concerned with our material wealth and accomplishments, but with experiencing each day, each moment, with joy."

Ann Marie's story deeply touched my heart, and begs the question of just what is prayer. In the following chapters, we will look at different types of prayer through the work and experiences of many individuals. Their stories have changed my awareness—as they will change yours—of the power available for help, guidance, and growth to each of us by opening our hearts through the process of prayer.

# *Two*

# THE ESSENCE OF PRAYER

**M**ost Americans believe strongly in the power of prayer and positive thought. They also believe that each person influences his or her own reality. Those are among the findings of a national survey commissioned by the Unity School of Christianity, which was founded more than a hundred years ago near Kansas City, Missouri. Unity offers one of the world's largest prayer services, of which we will hear much more later in this book.

According to the survey, nearly nine in ten persons, or eighty-eight percent, believe that prayer and meditation can have a positive effect on their emotional health. Nearly eight in ten, or seventy-nine percent, believe that prayer and meditation can positively influence their physical health. Eighty-five percent believe that praying for others has a beneficial effect. And seventy-seven percent believe that prayer and meditation facilitate a direct experience of God.

The national mail survey of 1,500 households was conducted in August 1993 by an independent organization, Fleishman-Hillard Research of St. Louis, Missouri. Respondents numbered 604, for a response rate of about forty percent, most of whom were above average in education and income. The results were weighted to reflect the national distribution of the adult population in terms of region, sex, and age.

The survey found that as people get older, they are more likely to believe that prayer and meditation positively affect their emotional health. Percentages were forty-two percent among those eighteen to thirty-nine years old; fifty-three percent among those forty to fifty-four years old, and fifty-seven percent among those fifty-five and older.

There were also regional differences: Southerners are more likely to believe strongly in the power of prayer to positively influence physical and emotional health, followed by Midwesterners.

As for positive thought, ninety-six percent of the respondents believe that what they think has an effect on their physical well-being. In addition, ninety-two percent believe that what they think can change the outcome of events in life, and ninety-two percent believe that a positive mental attitude can be "very effective" in helping to deal with life's challenges.

Are so many people right? Do prayer and positive thought wield significant influence over the course of our lives and the quality of our health?

The answer is a resounding yes. The respondents to the survey reflect the beliefs of average Americans, who speak from their own experiences. What's more, we can find plenty of evidence in support of those views in science, theology, and anecdotal testimony.

Prayer works. We are what we think and pray.

## Defining prayer

Prayer is an enormous source of power. It has been credited with great accomplishments and miraculous healings. Prayer is also a complex subject that acts rather like quicksilver. No matter how we try to define it and contain it, its true shape eludes us.

Essentially, prayer is an act of communing with God, or the Divine, or the Supernatural, or the Universal Mind—pick your term depending on your spiritual or religious outlook. Prayer has existed in numerous forms since the human race became conscious. It is fundamental to all religions; William James once noted that prayer "is the very soul and essence of religion." Yet, prayer thrives outside organized religion too. It is the essential link that helps us bridge two worlds—our mundane world and a transcendent reality. In that transcendent world, we see all things as being possible.

"Prayer is a spiritual activity that is often ineffable," says Rev. Richard L. Batzler, former national president of the Spiritual Frontiers Fellowship International. "Prayer is a power within us that is a dynamic release that can change the course of our day or even our lives. Prayer expresses our divine nature. It allows one to dialogue with God in a productive manner."[1]

## Types of prayer

The simplest and most common form of prayer is the *petition,* in which we ask for something for ourselves. The word "prayer" itself means to petition, coming from the Latin term *precarius,* which means "obtained by begging." Most of us make petitionary prayers on an almost daily basis, informally, whenever we want something to go right in life or when we want something to change.

The question of who or what is petitioned is a big one. Depending on religion and cultural background, we petition God, Goddess, the Divine, saints, angels, the ancestral dead, hosts of spirits, or even forces of nature.

Another common form of prayer is the *intercession,* in which we ask for help for another person. Petition and intercession, as we will see throughout this book, are instrumental in healing.

Other kinds of prayer are *thanksgiving, adoration, confession, lamentation, meditation, contemplation,* and *surrender.* Meditation and contemplation are mystical in nature. These kinds of prayers are instrumental in healing, especially healing into wholeness—the kind of healing that takes place on the level of the soul and in the inner chambers of the heart. Plato once observed that "if the head and the body are to be well, you must begin by curing the soul; that is the first thing. . . . The great error of our day in the treatment of the human body [is] that physicians separate the soul from the body."[2]

Prayer of surrender also plays an important role in healing. Rather than ask for something specific, the prayer of surrender turns the resolution entirely over to divine will. It asks nothing and accepts whatever is the outcome. Many people who pray regularly—and who have had stunning experiences with petitionary and intercessionary prayer—find that ultimately, the best and most effective prayer is one of surrender.

Daniel J. Benor, M.D., a psychiatrist, healer, and leading researcher in alternative healing, sees three levels of prayer. The first is an assertion of our will: "Heal dammit, heal." The second is prayer that attempts to understand illness and its underlying causes, and to learn the spiritual lessons from that. These lessons may relate not only to the person but to those around him or her and to future lives as well. The third level of prayer is surrender to God's will. "We don't have sufficient resources to answer the question about which level might be more effective, or whether they are equally effective," says Benor. "Different personalities might prefer one over the other. Maybe each is particularly effective for different problems."[3]

## Institutional views on prayer

From an early age, many of us learn rather rigid definitions and methods of prayer in church or perhaps at home. We are given proper ways to pray and proper things to say. We memorize prayers. We pray at certain times in certain postures—down on our knees or with heads bowed and eyes closed or with hands clasped. Sometimes these prayer rituals have meaning, and we can feel the universe move within us. Great things happen. More often than not, we feel little or no psychic connection to our ritualized prayers. They seem to have no real power—and then we wonder why prayers don't seem to be answered. But we don't change our rituals, because we've been taught that they're right, and deviation from them is wrong.

Prayer cannot be prescribed and packaged. Prayer is a living thing, but it does not live if we breathe no life into it from our hearts. Our concept of the Absolute is but a tiny fragment of the whole picture. Like an iceberg, most of it is submerged in mystery. Religions, with their hierarchies and rules, are products of human thought and politics. We project ourselves onto our religions, we make gods and angels in our own images, when in fact the Absolute lies beyond such concerns.

Boyce Batey, of whom I wrote in the introduction, echoed the sentiments of many people who have had their spiritual eyes opened by a mystical or profound spiritual experience. He said that afterward, he became less religious and far more spiritual. "I knew of a greater reality," he said. "Before the experience, I believed in God. After the experience, I no longer believed in God—I knew that God *is*."

Ultimately, prayer protocols and rules are arbitrary. What does matter is intent: that we pray out of love and with a pure and honest heart. Prayer sets powerful forces in motion.

## The substance of prayer

Anyone who has ever studied prayer—whether from an anthropological, sociological, theological, or scientific perspective—is at a loss to explain precisely what constitutes prayer. Most often, it is called an "energy." When we pray, especially for healing, we often get a sense of movement of energy, or of heat and light. Yet, prayer itself is not heat, nor is it light. If prayer is an energy, it exists in a form that cannot be measured by science as we know it. It is definitely nonlocal in nature. It has an effect at a distance—any distance, no matter how great. Nothing can block it or diminish it.

Prayer reinforces the idea that consciousness extends beyond the body. Yet, if it can affect things in the physical world, then prayer and these effects should be measurable. Prayer, says British plant physiologist Rupert Sheldrake, "clearly poses a challenge to the mechanistic view of the world. According to this view, there is no way that thoughts going on in your head, which at most create small electrochemical disturbances barely detectable a few inches from your head even by highly sensitive apparatus, could affect someone or something at a remote distance."[4]

## Prayer and morphogenetic fields

Prayer *can* be explained as a scientific phenomenon, asserts Sheldrake. The key rests on the notion that the mind is not confined to the brain—that consciousness is nonlocal.

Sheldrake is perhaps best-known for his work on the hypothesis of morphic resonance and morphogenetic fields, from the concept of "morphogenic fields" in developmental biology. Back in the 1920s morphogenic fields was a mathematical abstraction. Sheldrake's scientific credentials are impeccable. He was a scholar of Clare College, Cambridge, where he read natural sciences. He was a Frank Knox Fellow at Harvard University, where he studied philosophy and the history of science. He received his Ph.D. in biochemistry at Cambridge. In the early 1980s he set the scientific world on its ear by hypothesizing the existence of morphogenetic fields that act over time and space to organize the forms and behavior of all biological, chemical, and physical systems. The influence is exerted through morphic resonance, a sort of tuning-in process for cells that governs what they do.

Sheldrake's hypothesis, presented in his books *A New Science of Life* (1981) and *The Presence of the Past* (1984), created a storm of controversy among scientists because it raised questions about the supposed inviolability of physical laws, which exist outside of time. Morphogenetic fields, on the other hand, exist within time, and, furthermore, their effects are cumulative. Whereas orthodox science holds that an organism ceases to affect anything when it dies, under Sheldrake's hypothesis, the influence of an organism continues after death, because of the collective, cumulative morphogenetic fields. It's rather like the wheel of birth, death, and rebirth, in which all things are recycled and reborn anew.

So where does prayer fit into this hypothesis? According to Sheldrake, there is no end to morphogenetic fields, which also include behavioral fields, responsible for coordinating instinctive or learned behavior; mental fields, which organize mental activity; social fields, which organize social behavior; and so on. Thoughts and emotions are affected by fields.

Prayer, then, functions through mental morphogenetic fields, which act as a kind of extended mind. These would not equate with God or the Universal Mind, says Sheldrake, but rather are both an individual and collective mind field that can spread out over immense distances. These fields enable us to have connections with people, animals, and places that we know and care about, Sheldrake says. The extended mental fields are the context in which prayer works nonlocally.

It's helpful to understand definitions and descriptions of prayer and hypotheses as to how prayer functions. But these do not let us touch the power itself. We can only do that through direct experience.

# Three

# "WOULD MY NEXT MOVE BE MY LAST?"

We may believe that prayer has power, but most of us never expect to have to put it to severe test. Guy Riggs certainly didn't—until an accident one day on rocky cliffs above the Irish Sea left him stranded in the elements for twenty-six hours, facing the prospect of paralysis or death.

Prayer and positive thinking pulled him through the immediate crisis. Group prayer by others helped him to heal.

I met Guy in the summer of 1994 at Findhorn Foundation, a spiritual community located on the shores of Findhorn Bay in the Scottish Highlands. We were among the several hundred people who were participating in the weeklong summer solstice festivities.

Guy was residing at Findhorn Foundation, as part of a spiritual quest he had undertaken. Findhorn Foundation was founded in 1962 by Eileen and Peter Caddy and Dorothy Maclean, and it rose to fame due largely to Maclean's mediumistic communications with angels of nature. The angels—or devas, as some call them—enabled the trio to grow spectacular flowers and produce in a harsh and inhospitable terrain and climate. Of the three founders, only Eileen Caddy remains, and communication with angels has receded into the background.

Findhorn Foundation has sought to distinguish itself as a model "city of light." There is a residential community for people who wish to live in a cooperative, communal fashion. There is an ongoing program of lectures, workshops, and spiritual retreats. People from all over the world make pilgrimages to Findhorn. Some apply to live in tiny caravans on campus. Others come for spiritual refreshment and rejuvenation.

I first saw Guy at a circle dance one evening inside the foundation's rustic but elegant auditorium. I was among the observers, seated up in the bleachers, watching the hundred-or-so dancers on the floor. Even from a distance, Guy seemed to me to possess an unusual aura about him. He was of average height, lean with angular features and thinning brown hair. He looked to be in his late thirties. He was graceful and agile in the dance. He did not execute any unusual movements, but he emanated an energy, a vitality, that others around him did not have.

The following day, I shared a lunch table with him and learned he was from Walton-on-Thames in England. He told me the story about his accident and how he had fractured his back in a rock-climbing fall. In fact, doctors had told him he might never walk well again, let alone dance. I found that incredible, having watched him dance the night before. I asked Guy to share the details:

"I first arrived at Findhorn Foundation in May 1993 for a three-month program," he began. "In September, I decided to attend a foundation-run retreat on the island of Iona, off the western coast of Scotland. Iona is wild and rocky, and many visitors there have experienced a strange, even magical energy. A lot of artists have had great inspirations during or after stays on the island.

"I was bored by the retreat, to be honest. Whenever I go to the west coast of Scotland or to Ireland, I experience a lot of energy rushing up through me, and I just have to express it. On Iona, I expressed it by climbing rocks. I went out by myself and climbed some steep rocks by the bay. I didn't have any ropes, which was foolish. Still, I didn't think anything was going to happen.

"I climbed up this one slope that was nearly vertical. Going up is always easier than coming down, and on the way down I got into trouble. I wasn't sure whether I could make it. I thought, 'Well, as long as I can sort of move each step down safely, I know I can reverse out.'

"I leaned out over the cliff to look for a place to put my right foot. I was about forty or fifty feet above the beach. My right hand was on a shelf and my left hand was on this big jug-hold. All of sudden the jug-hold just came away.

"I fell about fifteen or twenty feet, landing on this large boulder. I hit my spine, fracturing my back, and rolled onto my stomach. I learned later that it was the top of my lumbar vertebrae that got fractured. I was in immediate, pretty bad pain, although it wasn't as bad as I would imagine a fractured back to feel. I wasn't screaming in uncontrollable agony, or anything like that. The main pain was mental. I knew very well that first-aid instruction says that if you have a broken back, don't move, because you can turn an abraded spinal cord into a broken spinal cord quite easily. I also feared that I might have done some damage to my organs, like my kidneys.

"For the first hour I couldn't feel my legs. When I summoned up the courage to twist my neck and look around, I was surprised at where my legs were. My left leg was bent at the knee, and the bottom half was pointing straight into the sky.

"I was in deep shock, but I was conscious all the time. I didn't do anything for a while, and then I realized I had to save myself from the tide, which would come in and drown me if I couldn't get to higher ground. And I had to get help.

"For one brief moment, I thought, 'Do I sort of lie here and die, or do I just hurl myself off this rock and down to the ground, so I'm over it quicker?' I thought about it and then I dismissed it. I couldn't accept just giving up. I had no sense of outrage at the situation. I was very calm. I don't know why this was. I felt very calm, very connected, and when night fell, I felt sort of peaceful."

"Did that surprise you, that calm?" I asked.

"Yes," Guy said. "Normally I'm not a calm person. But as soon as I landed, I felt calm. It was quite an altered state. Perhaps it was a mental self-defense mechanism. Panic for me usually involves making choices. And the choices are on one level important and on another level fairly trivial. At the end of the day, you're still going to get your meal at half past twelve, and it doesn't matter which choice you make, if you know what I mean. But with this situation, if I made the wrong choice, I could easily die.

"I had no choice but to escape the tide. I began to crawl along the rocks away from the water. I found I could move my legs, but the effort was awful. I didn't have much of a sense of where my legs were, or how they felt.

"So I crawled. The worst part of crawling was wondering whether the next move was going to be the one that severed my cord. That was unpleasant. But I said to myself, 'No, that's not going to happen.' I had to keep that positive thought in my mind. Gradually feeling in my legs came back as a tingling, which felt very strange and is hard to describe.

"I was able to crawl to the back of the bay, and then I looked around to try to find a way out of it. There wasn't a way that I could see. I realized I'd have to try to get up the cliff to avoid the tide. I looked around for the easiest place to start. I found a place and started crawling up it. But that turned into very, very steep grass, which I just inched my way across. Then the grass gave way to steep rock. Lucky for me, part of this rock had given way and fallen down, and it made a little shelf about four or five feet long and about a foot wide. I crawled onto it and just lay there. That I'd gotten there was a miracle in itself. I could see that the climbing above me was far, far too hard, and there was no way I was going to go any further up. There was no way to the right or to the left, either. So I just stayed there. The weather began to deteriorate as it got dark. It rained a little on and off. I worried about exposure. My body was actually maintaining its temperature quite well, but my limbs were extremely cold. And I was incredibly dehydrated."

"What went through your mind?" I asked.

"I never gave up hope," Guy said. "I played a lot of mind games. I did things like count back from very, very large numbers. I savored all the qualities of those numbers, and whether I knew someone who lived in a house with such and such a number, or something like that. I'd sing songs and say mantras. I did lots of the Om mantra, like a prayer. I did the three-part version, pronouncing all three syllables, *Ah-Oh-Mm.* It seemed to keep my internal body warmer than it might otherwise have been.

"Whenever I had judged a half-hour had passed—I wasn't carrying a watch—I let out some loud cries for help. I think they were loud. But I was quite winded, so it took a long time before I could shout well.

"I guessed I wouldn't be found. I figured the people I was staying with on the neighboring island of Mull probably wouldn't miss me until about eight or nine at night, if they missed me at all. I learned later that they'd assumed I'd missed the last ferry or had decided to stay on the island and not return to Mull. They were not worried when I did not return.

"I deliberately kept myself awake all night while I was on this ledge. The last thing I wanted to do was to fall asleep and roll off it. I also feared I might drift into unconsciousness and die. Playing the mind games and chanting the Om, I made it through the night.

"Throughout the next day there were fishing boats passing by. I'd make an effort to wave to them and shout, but nothing happened.

There were a couple of moments of despair. Once, just before I was found, there was a sailing boat that came very close to shore. It couldn't have been more than fifty yards away from the mouth of the bay. I yelled at the man aboard and waved, but he didn't notice me. I must admit I found myself cursing. He sailed on by, but I ended up saying, 'I love you, anyway!' and 'I forgive you!'

"I made a bargain with God," continued Guy. "I made myself some intentions: 'I will survive and I will live, and I will live well. These intentions, these affirmations were my prayer. There was none of this begging, 'Oh, God, please save me!' My prayer was my intentions to survive and live well. I kept thinking about the process of living after this was over, and that it might be hard.

"When it became apparent that I wasn't going to be spotted and rescued, I began to crawl back down the cliff I'd so painfully crawled up. I thought perhaps I'd made a mistake and there really was another way out. There wasn't, but I didn't know that. While I was going down, I was discovered by a man who was out walking on the road above the cliff. He summoned help, and he also found three other walkers who were in the vicinity, and asked them to come down and be with me. He realized the importance of that, but the people he asked didn't. They came down, took a look at me and they said, 'Oh, hello. Do you mind if we go?' At which point my show of remarkable togetherness dissolved instantly. I'd kept myself together emotionally for twenty-six hours, and here were these people who couldn't appreciate my situation. I couldn't cope. I got very emotional and so they stayed.

"After a long time and much inconsequential small talk, the Coast Guard arrived. They couldn't help me, so they summoned a helicopter from a nearby air base. The helicopter came, and I was airlifted out. I was taken first to a wee cottage hospital. They X-rayed me and determined that my back was broken. It was late at night by then. I remember hearing hard rain on the roof and thinking that if I were still on the cliff in that rain, I'd very quickly die. I was aware that I was taken in the nick of time. I took a shot of morphine somewhere in the night to help me sleep. I didn't really need it for pain. What I felt was more of an awareness than a shattering pain. I wasn't in agony.

"The next day I was moved to a hospital in Glasgow, where I was diagnosed with a nasty compaction break. They sent me to the newly opened Queen Elizabeth Center for National Spinal Injuries in Glasgow. I was offered the choice of bed rest or operation. The bed rest option would last for months—months and months. By that time, I was already appreciating how dangerous lying down immobile is for your body. It really does mess it up.

"So I opted for the operation. They operated on a Wednesday morning, just over a week after I fell. It was a long operation, four or five hours. I lost an awful lot of blood during it. They stiffened the spine with metal and bone from my pelvis. They said I would never be able to gain full flexibility of the spine. There was some question as to whether I'd be able to walk, or how easily or pain-free I could walk again.

"The day after the operation, the entire kitchen crew at Findhorn—the people I worked with—came to visit me, which really made me feel good. I found out that as soon as they'd heard about my accident, they started praying for me, individually and in groups. Every morning, there is a period of meditation and prayer at Findhorn. They prayed for me every day. I'm sure this helped me."

Guy continued the account of his recovery. "The hospital staff made a brace for me that was like a cage, and the following Tuesday afternoon they sat me up. Just being upright released an amazing amount of grief. I was also aware of how much weight I'd lost. I looked like a concentration camp victim. I couldn't believe it! I swear, I cried all evening.

"The following day I took my first steps. By the evening I was walking around unaided. By Thursday I could climb their stairs, which were a test as to whether or not you could leave the hospital. On Friday, I found a football and kicked it around.

"I remember my first trip otuside. It was sunny, beautiful weather in Glasgow. I staggered outside and found a tree. I was a bit shy of hugging it, but I just lay down under it and put my hands up to the trunk. It made me feel connected to it. From then on, my spiritual practice became saying 'thank you.' I said it every time I walked. 'Thanks for these steps.' That's still my practice.

"I left on the following Tuesday and went to stay at my brother's home in Lincolnshire. Walking even one hundred yards would kill me, and I'd need to rest for a couple hours. I couldn't stay upright for more than about an hour or two. When I ate food, my temperature would rise and I'd start feeling quite ill. That took a week or so to lessen, but it still happens to me now, nine months after the accident.

"I was determined to be active again, no matter how difficult it was. I did my first circle dance in October, exactly twenty-eight days after I fell. I did it gently, and even so it nearly killed me! I spent the whole next day in bed.

"On November fifth, I went out with a mountaineering club and did a ten-mile walk in the Black Mountains of Wales. I wasn't the last one up onto the top of the mountain either, though I felt like I was going to die at the end of the day!

"In December, I went back to Glasgow for a medical review. The doctors said they were well pleased and somewhat surprised at my recovery. They talked about taking the metal brace off. The idea of giving the cage up was my greatest challenge. It was a psychological and physical support to my whole back, which was still very weak. I wasn't prepared to give it up, and I carried on wearing it until a week into the new year.

"When the cage finally came off, I became very depressed and went through a bad period. I'd lost my status as a spinal-injuries patient. I went down and down. Finally, I realized that the only person who could pull me through this was myself, and I had to get myself together."

Guy was able to achieve this by undertaking a lot of inner work. In the spring of 1994, he returned to Findhorn Foundation.

I asked Guy how his experience had changed him.

"I'm still integrating it," he said. "I know there's a reason for it, and a reason why I lived. It's definitely strengthened my belief in God. I know I can call on that power whenever I need it. Nothing is impossible."

I was struck by Guy's use of the mantra Om, from Hinduism and Buddhism. As a prayer, Om is profound—it connects one to God as readily and as powerfully as any formal Christian prayer. Om (also spelled *Aum*) is the most sacred and comprehensive expression of spiritual knowledge. It is a symbol of form and a manifestation of spiritual power. It represents supreme consciousness, which encompasses and reveals the three states of waking, dreaming, and deep sleep (the unconscious).

According to the Upanishads, Om is the imperishable Brahman, which is the Supreme Reality and Truth, and ineffable peace and supreme good. The Self is one with Om. The Taittiriya Upanishad states that "He who meditates on Om attains to Brahman." This is comparable to the concept of the indwelling God or Christ consciousness; to connect with that is to connect with the transcendent, omnipresent God.

In yoga, Om is used as a mantra to pierce the material nature of the body in order to purify and bring the soul in touch with the Absolute. Om is a favored mantra of meditators, for it clears the mind and centers the consciousness.

For Guy, it was a prayer that formed a lifeline to the greatest power in the universe.

# Four

# Prayer, Psi, and Healing

To further our investigation of the healing power of prayer, we must probe the mysterious world of psi. *Psi* is a term for both extrasensory perception (ESP) and psychokinesis (PK). ESP includes telepathy, clairvoyance, clairaudience, and clairsentience; PK is the apparent influence of mind over matter through unexplained means. Examples of PK are levitation, movement of objects, luminosities, miraculous healings, bilocations, etc.

Psi phenomena are associated with both prayer and meditation. The literature of Western mystics describes clairvoyance, clairaudience, levitation, precognition, prophecy, and more as unsought byproducts of prayer. Some of these are described in more detail in the final chapters in the book *Prayer and the Modern Mystic,* which describes the miraculous healing of St. Teresa of Avila through mental prayer, and in *Prayer Power for the New Millennium.*

Here, we will take a look at what science can tell us about prayer and how it works, and about the relationship between prayer and psi.

Daniel J. Benor, M.D., one of the preeminent researchers in psi and healing, notes that psi phenomena "are clearly related to healing. Psychokinesis resembles healing, as both entail the mind influencing matter. In fact, healing may simply be PK on living things. Similarly, clairsentience appears to be the basis for psychic medical diagnosis and is probably the means by which healers know how to help healees. Telepathy, which can span vast distances, may prove to be an aspect of distant diagnosis and healing."[1]

Prayer, says Benor, "is a ritualized request for help or an acknowledgment of a connection to something higher than one's self. When it is a request for help, it overlaps with psi and ESP. When it is a connection with something higher, it moves into the realm of the mystical.

"I believe that prayer can bring about PK effects such as those associated with healing. The petitionary aspect of prayer may actually invoke the personal PK abilities of the person who does the praying, rather than activate any external forces. A person's faith can strengthen their ability to activate PK, or access levels of awareness where PK exists. Belief in saints or God may be of help to the person who prays but may not necessarily be a reality.

"On the other side of it, there are pray-ers who say they psychically sense the presence of helping guides such as from the angelic realms. We have evidence for both realities. Which reality applies, or is invoked, depends on the belief systems of the parties who are participating. Maybe it's not one versus the other, but both."[2]

## Psi or spiritual healing

Prayer is inextricably part of what Benor calls psi healing and others call spiritual healing or even faith healing. Benor defines two broad categories of healing: the first involves prayer or meditation conducted by an individual or a group; the second involves some version of a laying on of hands, such as an "energy transfer." Even in the second group, prayer is fundamental: most healers either pray or center themselves with some sort of prayerful meditation before they begin healing.

According to Benor, more than 141 controlled studies of psi healing have been done. More than half have yielded statistically significant results; that is, they provide evidence that supports the existence of a tangible relationship between psi and healing.

Benor became interested in psi healing when he visited a Reiki healer to see the process at work. "She did a laying on of hands on the chakras of a young man who had a cyst on one nipple," Benor said. "The healing lasted only half an hour. The cyst literally shrank. Where it had started out tender, it was not tender when the healing finished. She hadn't even touched the lesion itself."

This so intrigued him that he embarked on his own investigation of psi healing. He found the attitudes toward psi healing significantly friendlier in the medical establishment in the United Kingdom, where doctors increasingly refer patients to psi healers. Benor now resides there and conducts his own practice of psychotherapy and healing out of his London office. In 1988 he and his wife, Rita, founded the Doctor-Healer Network, an organization of healers, doctors, nurses, other health-care professionals, complementary therapists, and clergy. Participants meet regularly to discuss patients and research. The overall purpose of the network is "to promote the integration of spiritual healing into the practice of medicine in its broadest sense."

Benor is the author of an impressive five-volume project, *Healing Research: Holistic Energy Medicine and Spirituality,* which is a comprehensive survey of the scientific literature on spiritual healing from around the world. In this work, he defines psi healing as "a systematic, purposeful intervention by one or more persons aiming to help another living being (person, animal, plant, or other living system), by means of focused attention, hand contact, or 'passes' to improve their condition. This may involve the invocation of belief systems which include external agents such as God, Christ, other 'higher powers,' spirits, universal or cosmic forces or energies; special healing energies or forces residing in the healer; psychokinesis (mind over matter); or self-healing powers or energies latent in the healee."[3]

## Prayer in healing

Virtually all healers center themselves with some kind of prayer as they begin their work. Ask a healer who or what it is that performs the healing, and they will say it is not them: the healing comes from God or the universal life energy. They are merely the instruments for it.

Besides prayer, psi or spiritual healing involves positive thinking, visualization, affirmation, the channeling of the universal life energy, and the administration of magical or blessed medicines (such as the waters at miraculous healing sites). These methods have been used nearly universally at various times since the earliest recorded human history.

Religious faith and belief in healing are not necessary for healing to take place. The premise of psi or spiritual healing is that all living things are permeated and sustained by the universal life force. A depletion in this energy, or an imbalance in it, causes illness and disease. The depletion can be caused by poor diet or lifestyle habits and even negative attitudes and thoughts.

Ambrose Worrall, renowned healer with his wife, Olga, defined spiritual healing as "the art of restoring a person (or other living entity) to a condition of health by the use of powers usually attributed to the Supreme Being and various saints." He said spiritual healing is a natural phenomenon that works in accordance with natural laws and can be accomplished long-distance.

In healing, a transfer of the universal life force is made from its divine source to the patient via the healer, usually through the hands. The healer may or may not actually touch the patient. The energy transfer often is accompanied by such sensations as heat, tingling, electrical shock, or impressions of colors. The healer, who becomes a passive conduit for the healing energies, may feel a physical exit of something the consistency of heavy air. Many feel it through the hands; Worrall felt energy leave him through the solar plexus in long-distance healings. The patient often feels an infusion of energy. Some healings are instantaneous—even the disappearance of tumors and swellings— but many more require numerous treatments, some over a period of years. Each case seems to be unique and not necessarily dependent on the varying abilities and skills of the healers themselves. Even exceptional healers have cases that are slow to respond or that do not respond at all.

Gifted healers usually are born with their ability, though virtually anyone can develop it to some extent. The healing ability manifests along with psychic abilities.

Like prayer, we don't know much about the mechanisms by which spiritual healing takes place. Consciousness certainly plays a key role, which means that spiritual healing is nonlocal and multidimensional. The process of healing may not be a matter of "how" but of "why": the need for a healing exists, and the consciousness selects a path to effect it.

## Altered states

Many healers work in an altered state of consciousness. In the 1960s, psychologist Lawrence LeShan, in research with healers, found that the healers could not adequately describe the process of healing but did describe shifting into a different reality, a state of consciousness he termed the "clairvoyant reality." It is a shift in one's metaphysical understanding of the world. It is similar to, but not identical to, mystical states that occur in all cultures around the world, and the shamanic state of consciousness.

For about eighteen months, LeShan experimented with various meditation techniques until he began to experience this shift of consciousness himself. He discovered that attaining the clairvoyant reality improves with practice and can be controlled to some extent, but remains largely unpredictable and unreliable. He also discovered that while in this state himself, others with whom he worked reported physical or psychological changes that seemed to benefit them. Furthermore, he could teach others how to reach the clairvoyant reality and awaken their healing powers.

Experiments by others have shown that brain-wave patterns change during spiritual healing. As the healer goes into an altered state, the brain waves change from beta (waking consciousness) to alpha (a lightly altered state) to theta (a deeper altered state characteristic of many mystical states). Olga Worrall could even achieve the delta stage, which is deep sleep. As the healer's brain waves change, so do those of the patients.

## Prayer in the laboratory

Most of the research on psi or spiritual healing and the effects of prayer has fallen within parapsychology. A factor in experiments that complicates the controls involved and can also make results difficult to assess is called the experimenter effect. This is the unwitting influence of the experimenter to make the results fit his or her expectations or beliefs.

The experimenter effect may manifest in various ways. For example, the experimenter may communicate telepathically to the subject.

Or, especially in cases where the subject is a plant or simple organism, the experimenter may unknowingly exert PK. The experimenter effect conforms with the quantum mechanics principle that the observer alters his or her environment merely by the act of observing.

The experimenter effect has been known for a long time. It was observed in psychical research as early as the 1930s. Before that, it was noticed in psychology, in the tendency of patients and therapists to establish a seemingly telepathic rapport.

The experimenter effect has been studied and tested by some parapsychologists. Researchers with a negative bias toward a particular hypothesis will tend to get results negating it, while researchers who believe in the hypothesis will tend to get results validating it. Emotions and attitudes toward subjects also have an influence. With that in mind, let's take a look at some of the significant laboratory research done on prayer.

In the 1950s, the Reverend Franklin Loehr, a chemical engineer who founded the Religious Research Foundation, in Los Angeles, conducted a series of controlled experiments on the power of prayer on seeds and seedlings. Loehr took several groups of seeds, usually corn or wheat, and planted them in identical soil in two identical pans. They were given equal amounts of water and light. Experimenters then prayed over one pan for a faster-than-usual germination and growth. The seeds in the second pan were ignored. Sometimes a third pan was included in the experiments; the prayers for it were negative—to retard growth. In some of the experiments, the prayers were directed to the soil or to the water, rather than the seeds themselves. Loehr found that the seeds that received the positive prayers usually sprouted faster and grew more quickly than those that had either no prayer or negative prayer.

In all, Loehr conducted 700 experiments using 150 persons as experimenters and involving 27,000 seeds. Increased growth rates ranged from 30 percent to 200 percent. Similar results were obtained with silkworm eggs and ivy cuttings. Loehr published his research in *The Power of Prayer on Plants* (1969). The scientific community discounted Loehr's research because he and his assistants had no scientific training and used rather crude methods to measure growth. Nonetheless, his work cannot be ignored.

Meanwhile, in England, some startling discoveries were being made about the effects of human thought on plants. The discoveries were almost accidentally made by a husband and wife team, George De La Warr, a psychically gifted civil engineer, and Marjorie De La Warr, an osteopath. The De La Warrs were approached by a small group of British doctors who were interested in experimenting with the alleged healing powers of radionics using plants. Radionics involves the radiation of energies by mechanical devices.

The De La Warrs were successful in affecting the germination and growth rates of plants with such devices. After three years of intense work, they then stumbled upon a shattering realization: that a *human factor* was inextricably bound up in the results of their experiments. For instance, seedlings planted in vermiculite that assistants *believed* had been treated to enhance growth—but in fact had not—grew as if they had been in treated vermiculite.

It seemed like a miracle: human thought could influence cell formation. All one had to do to get plants to flourish was ask them to do so. The De La Warrs had encountered the experimenter effect. And what an effect!

When De La Warr described this experiment to one of Great Britain's leading physicists and suggested that a universal energy could be evoked by the proper attunement of one's thoughts, he was told curtly: "I do not believe you, Mr. De La Warr. If you can affect the number of atoms in a growing plant by your thought process, we must revise our concept of what constitutes matter."

"Indeed we must," said De La Warr, "even if such revision poses a whole overhaul of existing knowledge. How, for instance, could this energy be incorporated into mathematical equations? What would happen to the law of the conservation of energy?"[4]

George De La Warr published an article, "Blessing Plants to Increase Their Growth," in *Mind and Matter,* his own journal. He invited readers to validate his results. He outlined a fifteen-step procedure that called for holding bean seeds and reverently blessing them in accordance with one's faith or denomination. The readers loved this, but the Roman Catholic Church did not. The Church scolded De La Warr in a letter, stating that no one below the rank of deacon could perform a blessing. Mere lay persons could only ask the Creator to perform a blessing. To placate the Church, De La Warr gave a new euphemistic name to his experiment: "Increasing the Rate of Plant Growth by the Mental Projection of an Undefined Energy."

Other studies have been conducted by other researchers with healers who prayed over seeds, plants, and water for plants. Some of the best-known were done with Olga and Ambrose Worrall.

Both Worralls had manifested psychic and healing ability at very young ages. Throughout her healing career, Olga never understood the true nature of healing, but could only describe its conditions. She knew the healing came not from herself, but from a higher power. She said gifted healers are biologically constructed to act like battery chargers: they take in the high-voltage energy of God and transform it into energy that can be used by living things. The process is aided by spiritual beings.

Neither Olga nor Ambrose ever studied medicine; Olga said technical knowledge would only confuse her. She excelled at intuitive diagnosis, clairvoyantly seeing afflicted parts of the body and knowing what to do to help them. The information came to her unbidden; all she did was quiet herself and let the healing take its own course. Prayer was an essential part of the healing, as were love, compassion, and a wholehearted desire to see the patient healed.

The Worralls had many spectacular and instantaneous cures, including tumors that shrank to nothing under their touch. Other healings required regular treatment over a period of time, some up to years. Some patients were not healed, but these were in the minority. No two cases were ever the same.

The Worralls believed strongly that science must support religion, and so they participated in numerous laboratory experiments. In various tests, Olga Worrall energized water, changing its viscosity and electrical properties; she also created wave patterns in cloud chambers.

One particular experiment involving the growth rate of rye grass yielded impressive results, especially since both Worralls prayed at a distance. Researcher Robert N. Miller planted rye grass and kept it under constant conditions of light, temperature, and water. He measured its growth rate, which was about 0.006 inch per hour (never exceeding 0.010 inch per hour). During the experiment, the Worralls, who were six hundred miles away, held the grass seedlings in their thoughts one night at nine P.M., which was their customary evening prayer time. One hour later, they then prayed for the grass by visualizing it growing rapidly in white light.

The growth rate of the grass jumped eighty-four percent. Electronic sensing devices showed that until nine P.M., the growth rate was 0.00625 inch. At nine P.M., it began to increase steadily, and by eight A.M., it had reached 0.0525 inch per hour. Over the next forty-eight hours, the growth rate declined, but never returned to its original level.

In another experiment conducted by Miller, he used a cloud chamber to see if Olga Worrall's healing could generate visible particles. The chamber was a glass cylinder with an aluminum bottom and a viewing glass at the top. Alcohol was introduced to the chamber, and then the cylinder was placed on a block of dry ice. This produced an alcohol mist. Any high-energy atomic particles that passed through the mist would be visible as vapor trails.

Worrall held the cylinder and treated it as though it were a patient receiving healing. Within the chamber, wave motions of vapor trails appeared. Some kind of "energy" seemed to be passing through the mist. Worrall was even able to produce turbulence within the chamber at a distance of six hundred miles.

Other tests showed that when Worrall was in her healing state, her brain waves were at the delta level, the state of deep sleep—yet she was fully conscious and felt at her best. The moment of healing occurred when she and the patient tuned in to each other's wavelength. At that moment, the patient registered changes in brain-wave lengths. Other changes observed in Worrall included the extension of her energy field to eighteen feet around her and increases in energy flowing from her hands during healing.

More recent experiments have examined the effect of meditation, prayer, and psi healing on the immune system. Laboratory studies have shown that meditation lowers respiration, heart rate, blood pressure, and lactase, the latter of which is a chemical in the blood associated with strenuous activity and stress. The alpha state of consciousness has been shown to benefit the immune system. Periods of prayer, in which the pray-er relaxes in an alpha state of consciousness, can also have the same effects as meditation.

Researchers also are investigating how psi or spiritual healing affects brain waves and immune system activities. As we saw earlier, healers—who center themselves with prayer—show a marked change in brain-wave activity when they heal.

Johrei (pronounced Jo-ray) is a type of psi or spiritual healing that was originated in Japan in the mid-1930s by a businessman, Mokichi Okada, who became known as Meishu-sama to followers of the Johrei Fellowship. He turned to a spiritual path following the ruination of his business in the depression of the 1930s and the death of his wife and child during childbirth. Meishu-sama received a series of divine revelations for a new age and major world changes that would happen first.

He conceived of Johrei, which could help humanity make the necessary changes in consciousness in order to make the transition to the new age and to eliminate suffering. Johrei is now practiced by about one million people around the world in about fifty countries.

Like Reiki, Therapeutic Touch, and other "energy transfer" techniques, Johrei is a harnessing of the divine, immutable energy of the universe for improvement of physical and spiritual health. It places great importance on prayer. No touching is required; the Johrei healer, or channel, transmits energy at a distance through the hands, usually one raised hand at a time.

Research by the Johrei Fellowship shows that during a Johrei session, both channel and recipient experience alpha brain-wave activity. Blind tests have been done to try to screen out the experimenter effect; recipients were placed behind screens without knowing whether and when Johrei was being administered to them.

More interestingly, other experiments show that persons who receive Johrei daily for a period of several months have a marked increase in natural killer (NK) cells, a type of T-cell that is part of the body's immune system and which attacks viruses and bacteria that enter the body. NK-cells were discovered in 1974.

Blood samples taken from five Johrei subjects showed that their NK-cell levels were two to three times higher than normal when they received Johrei every day for four months. One subject's level increased by eight times.

This research, still in its early stages at the time this book goes to press, is ongoing in university laboratories. It may lead to important advancements in our efforts to fight all kinds of diseases, especially AIDS.

Meishu-sama believed that Johrei is best administered by someone with "deep faith." Johrei always begins with a solemn prayer to God. The channel maintains a prayerful attitude throughout the session (the average length of a session is about twenty minutes). According to

Meishu-sama, "The long-term benefits of Johrei are commensurate with the depth of the administrator's faith, and also with his sincerity and acceptance of God's love. That is why Johrei is more effective when it is given by one whose soul is relatively unclouded and who lives the faith he really feels. The purer and stronger the soul, the greater the blessings that Johrei will bring."[5]

## The Spindrift experiments

There have been numerous scientific studies of psi and healing (although psi healing frequently involves prayer), but very little scientific work has been devoted exclusively to the effects of prayer on healing. Prayer may be a mainstay of religion, and of daily life, yet there has been a marked lack of effort to test its power, especially to heal. Like the power of love, prayer is an orphan in the world of scientific experimentation.

Since 1975, pioneering work in this field has been carried out by a small nonprofit group called Spindrift, Inc. Spindrift's experiments demonstrate that prayer is effective, and furthermore, that nondirected prayer gets better results than directed prayer.

Spindrift's work has roused plenty of controversy in both religious and scientific circles. Much to their chagrin, the Spindrift people have found themselves spurned on almost all fronts, even by their own church, the Church of Christ, Scientist.

## Background

In 1975 a small group of Christian Scientists came together to research the effect of consciousness on the material world. They were interested in whether there was a power to prayer other than that of human faith (the placebo effect). They also were interested in the experimenter effect. Both placebo and experimenter effects are essentially mild forms of faith, Spindrift says.

The primary researchers have been a father and son team, Bruce and John Klingbeil, respectively.

In the words of John Klingbeil, "Spindrift's research arose from one fundamental conviction: that quality and quantity are unified on some basic level, that science and Christianity are one in essence although divergent in approach, that each reveal the mind of the Creator."[6]

The early, simple experiments done by the group seemed to support the notion that consciousness does have an effect on the material world and that that effect is to move organic and inorganic systems in the direction of greater order. Seeds were stressed by undersoaking, oversoaking, or soaking in salty water. Those seeds that were prayed over germinated significantly faster than control seeds that were not prayed over. Similarly, a group of stressed soybeans showed that the same prayer had different effects, depending on the needs of the seeds. Undersoaked beans retained more water than control beans, and oversoaked beans gave off more water than the controls.

In 1977 Bruce Klingbeil informed the Christian Science board of directors about the experimental work. The board responded by banning him from conducting research that conflicted with church doctrine that prayer could not be scientifically proven. From 1977 to 1983, the experiments were conducted by John Klingbeil, who was not recognized by the church as a Christian Science practitioner. In 1983 Bruce Klingbeil was expelled from the Christian Science healing ministry, and he resumed his work.

In 1981 father and son had formed Spindrift, Inc., as a nonprofit, charitable organization to help support the research, but funding proved to be elusive. The work continued because a small group of highly committed individuals were able to work on a low budget out of their homes.

By 1987 Spindrift realized that its work with simple organisms such as seeds and yeast cells was not going to attract much attention. Thus, it devised a new, repeatable, anyone-can-do-it test, "a test which clearly demonstrated the power of thought apart from the mediation of the human nervous system," the Klingbeils said. The new tests involved visual imagery.

In 1993 Spindrift published its work in a volume called *The Spindrift Papers*. The experiments continue.

## Holy thought

Spindrift hypothesized that a "holy state of consciousness" was the driving force of spiritual healing and that in virtually everyone a sufficient level of this consciousness exists to exert an influence; the individual acts as a focusing agent rather than as a source of the holiness.

Spindrift took into consideration the emphasis given to proportion by Christian Science founder Mary Baker Eddy. The underlying idea was that health and harmony are in proportion to one's "holiness"— that is, one's embodiment of the attributes or qualities of God, one's living and loving the Ten Commandments and the Sermon on the Mount, and so on. The "holier" one was in this regard, the greater the power of one's prayer. This view is akin to the one arrived at independently by Meishu-sama, pertaining to Johrei.

Other proportions also would affect the power of prayer: the quality of thought, the quantity of thought, the strength of one's awareness of what was prayed for, and the values used to measure the experiments.

Spindrift had to define prayer in terms that could be studied by the scientific method. Thus, God's response to prayer was viewed as universal and impartial, and God's grace was a matter of law rather than selective response. As for defining prayer in terms acceptable to the Christian community, Spindrift treated prayer like ice cream: the various Christian denominations are like flavors. Spindrift chose to research ice cream and not flavors. "That is, we had to find a way to do for prayer what medical research had done for drugs. We had to separate the power and grace of God from the placebo effect of human faith," the Klingbeils said. The way Spindrift solved these problems was to measure in reference to pattern: prayer and God's love would support the pattern (or big picture) of every identity.

## Directed versus nondirected prayer

Early tests by Spindrift demonstrated the overall efficacy of prayer. But in tests with mold, Spindrift found that nondirected prayer works better than directed prayer. Directed prayer, or "nonqualitative thought," is goal-directed and pushes a biological system in a specific direction determined by the healer. Nondirected prayer, or "qualitative thought," or "holy thought," is a state of consciousness that focuses on the qualities and attributes of God without trying to direct specific changes in a biological system. The result is that the system changes toward the norm.

In the tests, mold in a dish was stressed with an alcohol rinse, which retards its growth. Strings divided the dishes in half. One half received directed prayer versus no prayer at all. In other dishes, one half received nondirected prayer versus no prayer at all. Directed prayer did not affect the growth of the mold, but the mold that received nondirected prayer grew.

Holy prayer, as Spindrift calls nondirected prayer that embodies the qualities of God, the Ten Commandments, and the Sermon on the Mount, "seems to get results no matter what formulation it is expressed in. Prayer is of the heart no matter what kind of language the mind uses to express it. That seems to be the bottom line. If it is in your heart to think of a soybean, a yeast cell, or a human being in terms of the Qualities of God, you are going to have a spiritualizing effect, a healing effect, on that soybean, that yeast cell, or that human being."[7]

Spindrift declines to speculate how one develops a God-inspired consciousness to facilitate the healing power of prayer. "This is where salvation, redemption, the way of the cross, the search for God, comes in. Spindrift leaves questions such as those to the churches. We only measure the results of qualitative thinking. We don't presume to be theologians and tell you the best way to pursue the goal."[8]

Not all tests with holy thought/prayer worked as one might expect. While holy prayer helped the growth of wheat and rye seeds, it actually inhibited the growth of triticale seeds. Spindrift opines that "the moral and spiritual side of the universe disapproves of this new genetic creation."[9]

That's an interesting result, but do we have the experimenter effect here? Perhaps the Christian Science background of the researchers poses an unwitting bias against anything that seems to be contrary to the natural order.

Spindrift also said it found evidence of a patterning effect that involves a larger picture than a single organism. It is by definition a "loving form of consciousness" that must be aware of a large amount of information. What's more, they also found evidence of a "mental force" that works to cover up the evidence of the patterning power. This is the equivalent of the defense mechanism in psychology and the devil in theology—i.e., a force that opposes holy prayer and works to neutralize or negate it.

Despite these and other intriguing results, it is difficult to give a wholesale endorsement to nondirected prayer over directed prayer. Prayer seems to be unpredictable in effect; even Spindrift acknowledges that healers cannot control the outcome of their prayer. People have healed with the benefit of both kinds of prayer. Directed prayer may be more appropriate in some cases. Larry Dossey, M.D., a leading researcher on spiritual healing and on prayer, notes that as Christian Scientists, the Spindrift researchers may be more introspective and passive and thus have a natural preference for nondirected prayer.

Benor finds Spindrift's results "tantalizing yet frustrating." Flaws in procedures cloud conclusions; nonetheless, the results show promise in an area of research that bears further investigation.

## General health benefits of prayer

The effect of prayer habits in boosting overall health and well-being can be seen in studies that look at the relationship between religion and social ties and health. Literally hundreds of studies have been done over the last two centuries, yet the findings remain largely ignored by the medical establishment. Jeffrey S. Levin, Ph.D., an epidemiologist and associate professor in the Department of Family and Community Medicine at Eastern Virginia Medical School, in Norfolk, Virginia, collects, evaluates, and publishes this data in an effort to bring it to the attention of medical practitioners and move it out of the margins of health care. Levin was awarded two grants by the National Institutes of Health to pursue scientific research on the effects of religion on health and aging.

Epidemiology is the study of the cause and effect of disease and illness assessed across a population. Studies show that religion seems to have a positive impact on cardiovascular disease, hypertension, stroke, cancer, colitis, enteritis, dozens of other illnesses, overall mortality, general health, and self-rated health. It must be noted, however, that these findings do not constitute *proof* of a consistent, positive impact of religion on health, because it is virtually impossible to separate out the effects of other factors such as heredity, environment, social influences, and psychodynamics. Also some religious groups are stricter than others in terms of dictating health-related behavior via moral codes and dietary rules.

However, the evidence of a positive effect is convincing. "We see a trend that where there is more religiosity, there is better health," says Levin.

The evidence does not point to any one religion or denomination as being better than others in terms of influence on health. Nor does it matter how one specifically practices religion, in terms of the frequency of worship, prayer, ritual, social contact, and such. It only matters that one does. "What matters is that people have some type of faith that they engage in on a regular basis, and that gives meaning and order to their lives," says Levin.

Levin does opine that participation in a religious group may be more beneficial than a solitary pursuit of religion because of various reinforcing social factors. For example, there may be some particular benefit to be derived from a group consciousness created by ritual and worship—a collective thought-form that builds up and precipitates down to the individual. (Group consciousness and collective thought-forms are created by prayer groups and circles—see Chapter 7.) However, that does not mean that one's health cannot benefit from solitary religious practice.

Levin cites a number of hypotheses to explain how and why religion impacts health:

*Psychosocial effects.* Religious involvement fosters a sense of belonging, social support, and convivial fellowship, all of which seem to buffer the adverse effects of stress and anger, and also perhaps help trigger psychoneuroimmunological pathways.

*Psychodynamics of beliefs.* Particular religious beliefs foster peacefulness, self-confidence, and a sense of purpose. Again, these can buffer against the detrimental effects of stress.

*Psychodynamics of rites.* Public and private practice of rituals of worship—such as prayer—can "ease anxiety and dread, defeat loneliness, and establish a sense of being loved and appreciated," according to Levin. These, plus the actual physiological markers of emotional arousal, are associated with health and well-being.

*Psychodynamics of faith.* The mere belief in God, the Godhead, or the Divine is health-enhancing. Various scriptures promise health and healing to the faithful, which may create a sort of emotional placebo effect in expectation.

*Superempirical influences.* Levin uses the term "superempirical" to describe a pantheistic, discarnate force or power, also called the universal life force, prana, chi, orgone, subtle energies, etc. This power affects the etheric and astral bodies. Religious practice such as prayer may facilitate access to, or activation of, this power for healing effect.

*Supernatural influences.* Religion fosters faith in a transcendent Being who bestows health and healing, inner peace, and sense of purpose.

We can see that scientific studies have much to tell us about prayer and how it works. To see these factors more in action on the human level, we must examine the power of prayer within the context of the power of thought.

# Five

# PRAYER AND THE POWER OF THOUGHT

For Charles and Myrtle Fillmore, Midwesterners who settled in Kansas City, Missouri, prayer was the driving force of their lives. They both had experienced the miraculous healing power of prayer firsthand. Myrtle was spiritually healed of tuberculosis, after doctors gave up on her. Charles had healed himself of a withered leg, which actually grew in length. Their experiences lit a bonfire inside them, and they dedicated the rest of their lives to a spiritual path and to helping others along their spiritual paths. In 1889, they founded Unity, a religious organization that serves people of all faiths, now known as the Unity School of Christianity. Through its threefold program of ministry, public education, and prayer, Unity has helped millions of people around the world experience their own miracles.

Unity took root in the fertile ground plowed by the New Thought movement of the nineteenth century, which preached the effectiveness of "mental science," or the power of right thought, affirmation, and prayer. About twenty or so years before the Fillmores had their eyes opened, Mary Baker Eddy made discoveries that led her to found the Church of Christ, Scientist. Eddy had suffered an early life of invalidism and had pursued various cures and treatments, including magnetic mental healing. She was disillusioned with these and became convinced that the only true healing comes from God. In 1866 she fell on icy pavement and suffered severe internal injuries. In bed and near death, she turned to the Bible for solace, and was struck by Matthew 9:1–8, in which Jesus tells a paralyzed man to "take up your bed and go home." Eddy suddenly realized that illness was an illusion and could be overcome. She recovered and, what's more, became a healer. She preached that there was no healing agent other than unity with God.

The Fillmores' independent discovery of the healing power of prayer began with Myrtle. Born Myrtle Page on August 6, 1845, in Pagetown, Ohio, to a Methodist family, she was raised to consider herself an invalid with an inherited tendency toward tuberculosis. Indeed, her health mirrored her self-image, and she was frail and sickly much of her early life.

After college, Myrtle became a schoolteacher. When she was about thirty years old, she was so ill with tuberculosis and malaria that she moved to Denison, Texas, in hopes that the warmer, drier climate would help her condition. There she opened a small private school. She joined an informal group of young persons who gathered together regularly to discuss philosophy and literature and read poetry. Another member of this group was Charles Fillmore, a railroad clerk.

A romance blossomed between the two, and they were married in 1881. Charles pursued a career in business. They moved about the country. Three sons were born. Their finances went up and down. Myrtle's health remained poor. Her chronic tuberculosis caused her to seek medical remedy after remedy, to no avail.

In the mid-1880s, the family moved to Kansas City, Missouri.

Charles and Myrtle Fillmore pursued mutual interests in religion and metaphysics, learning about Buddhism, Brahmanism, Theosophy, and Rosicrucianism, among other topics.

One spring night in either 1885 or 1886 (the exact date is unknown), the Fillmores attended a lecture given by Dr. E. B. Weeks, who came to Kansas City to talk about New Thought. Myrtle was desperately ill with tuberculosis; in fact, her doctors had told her there was nothing more they could do for her, and she would not have long to live if she remained in the climate of Kansas City. A friend had recommended Weeks to her in the hopes that she might learn something that would help improve her condition. The Fillmores didn't know much about the New Thought movement, although they were familiar with Christian Science and its offshoots. Myrtle thought she didn't have anything to lose by attending the lecture.

It proved to be a life-changing night. Weeks made one statement that rang in Myrtle's ears and stuck with her for the rest of her life: *"I am a child of God and therefore I do not inherit sickness."* To Myrtle, taught from early childhood that she had inherited an invalid life, it was a divine revelation. She was never the same again.

Thus inspired by her revelation, Myrtle threw out her medicines and began praying. She prayed and prayed. Hourly, day and night. Two years later, she was completely healed. The tuberculosis was gone. For the remainder of her life—she died on October 6, 1931—she was healthy and vigorous.

By her own account, Myrtle said the key to her discovery of self-healing was that we can communicate with the divine intelligence that exists in all forms, including the body. Her description of how she went about this should be scrutinized and taken to heart by anyone who sincerely desires to be healed. She wrote:

> Life has to be guided by intelligence in making all forms. The same law works in my own body. Life is simply a form of energy, and has to be

guided and directed in man's body by his intelligence. How do we communicate intelligence? By thinking and talking, of course. Then it flashed upon me that I might talk to the life in every part of my body and have it do just what I wanted. I began to teach my body and got marvelous results.

I told the life in my liver that it was not torpid or inert, but full of vigor and energy. I told the life in my stomach that it was not weak or inefficient, but energetic, strong, and intelligent. I told the life in my abdomen that it was no longer infested with ignorant thoughts or disease, put there by myself and by doctors, but that it was all athrill with the sweet, pure, wholesome energy of God. I told my limbs that they were active and strong. I told my eyes that they did not see themselves but that they expressed the sight of Spirit, and that they were drawing on an unlimited source. I told them that they were young eyes, clear, bright eyes, because the light of God shone right through them. I told my heart that the pure love of Jesus Christ flowed in and out through its beatings and that all the world felt its joyous pulsation.

I went to all the life centers in my body and spoke words of Truth to them—words of strength and power. I asked their forgiveness for the foolish, ignorant course that I had pursued in the past, when I had condemned them and called them weak, inefficient, and diseased. I did not become discouraged at their being slow to wake up, but kept right on, both silently and aloud, declaring words of Truth, until the organs responded. And neither did I forget to tell them that they were free, unlimited Spirit. I told them that they were no longer in bondage to the carnal mind; that they were not corruptible flesh, but centers of life and energy omnipresent.

Then I asked the Father to forgive me for taking His life into my organism and there using it so meanly. I promised Him that I would never, never again retard the free flow of that life through my mind and my body by any false word or thought; that I would always bless it and encourage it with true thoughts and words in its wise work of building up my body temple; that I would use all diligence and wisdom in telling it what I wanted it to do.

*I also saw that I was using the life of the Father in thinking thoughts and speaking words, and I became very watchful as to what I thought and said* [italics are mine].

I did not let any worried or anxious thoughts into my mind and I stopped speaking gossipy, frivolous, petulant, angry words. I let a little prayer go up every hour that Jesus Christ would be with me and help me to think and speak only kind, loving, true words. I am sure that He is with me because I am so peaceful and happy now. . . .

I want everybody to know about this beautiful, true law, and to use it. It is not a new discovery, but when you use it and get the fruits of health and harmony, it will seem new to you, and you will feel that it is your own discovery.[1]

Myrtle's neighbors could not help but notice that she was a new woman. Word spread about her miraculous recovery and how she did it without medical help. Others who were ill or afflicted came to her seeking help.

Among the first was an Irishman named Caskey, who was crippled and had to walk with the aid of crutches. He was skeptical that prayer and thought could heal him, but, as Myrtle had been two years earlier, he was desperate to try anything. The two would meet and discuss Myrtle's new philosophy of wholeness, and they would pray together. Following the example of Jesus and the paralyzed man, Myrtle would tell Caskey to put down his crutches and walk. Repeatedly, he would deny the possibility, saying, "How do I know I can walk?" Myrtle patiently would reinforce affirmative thoughts and prayers.

One day, Caskey put down his crutches and walked, never to take them up again.

Similarly, Myrtle helped a woman to be healed of asthma and helped a young boy blinded by cataracts to see again. After a single session, the boy regained partial vision, and in a short while, the cataracts disappeared altogether. There were many others. Myrtle had become a healer, and her fame spread.

Charles, despite his spiritual interests, also remained skeptical for a while. He was a practical businessman, science-minded, and not one to jump on faith bandwagons. He later said, "Although I was a chronic invalid and seldom free from pain, the doctrine did not at first appeal to me."

Charles, who was born on August 22, 1854, in St. Cloud, Minnesota, suffered from a seemingly incurable affliction. He was ten years old when he dislocated his right hip in a skating accident. Rheumatism apparently set in, and the leg grew steadily worse.

Then a nightmare began: a steady stream of doctors attempted cures that proved to be worse than the affliction itself. Charles was subjected to every experimental remedy of the day. He was bled, leeched, cupped, lanced, seasoned, blistered, and roweled. Doctors created six running sores on his leg to draw out the alleged poisons within. Every doctor marveled at how Charles had survived the ministrations of the previous doctor, only to add to his agony.

As a result of the abuse, the hip socket was destroyed. Two large tubercular abscesses developed at the top of the leg that doctors said would kill him. The leg stopped growing and could not be moved. Charles was bedridden as an invalid for a year.

In all, the disease took two years to run its course. It was so violent that, at times, Charles thought he would die. When the misery was over at last, the leg was withered. From the hip to the knee, the flesh was a glossy adhesion with little sensation. Furthermore, Charles's entire right side had been adversely affected. His right ear was deaf, and his right eye was weak.

Charles was forced to walk on crutches. He wore a four-inch cork-and-steel extension on his shriveled leg. He was in chronic pain for twenty-five years—until he witnessed Myrtle's healing of tuberculosis.

Myrtle's healing was hard for Charles to believe, but he could not deny what he could see with his own eyes. It stimulated him to undertake an in-depth study of prayer, thought, and healing. All the teachers he read said the same thing: God is omniscient and accessible to everyone. Charles wrote:

I said to myself, "In this babel I will go to headquarters. If I am Spirit and this God they talk so much about is Spirit, we can somehow communicate, or the whole thing is a fraud."

I then commenced sitting in the silence every night at a certain hour and tried to get in touch with God. There was no enthusiasm about it; no soul desire, but a cold calculating business method. I was there on time every night and tried in all conceivable ways to realize that my mind was in touch with the Supreme Mind.

In this cold, intellectual attitude one can easily understand why I did not seem to get any conscious result, but I kept at it month after month, mentally affirming words that others told me would open the way, until it got to be a habit and I rather enjoyed it.[2]

Then something happened. Charles noticed his dreams changed. They became "exceedingly realistic," and he soon realized that "there was a wider intelligence manifesting in my sleep than I seemed to possess in the waking state, and it flashed over me one day that this was the mode of communication that had been established in response to my desire for information from headquarters."

Much of the information Charles received in his dreams was prophetic. The dream prophecies continued for the rest of his life. Through his prayerful efforts, Charles had become a prophet and a mystic.

Meanwhile, he began to heal. He wrote years later:

When I began applying the spiritual treatment, there was for a long time slight response in the leg, but I felt better, and I found that I began to hear with the right ear. Then gradually I noticed that I had more feeling in the leg. Then as the years went by the ossified joint began to get limber, and the shrunken flesh filled out until the right leg was almost equal to the other. Then I discarded the cork-and-steel extension and wore an ordinary shoe with a double heel about an inch in height. Now the leg is almost as large as the other, the muscles are restored, and although the hip bone is not yet in the socket, I am certain that it soon will be and that I shall be made perfectly whole.

I am giving minute details of my healing because *it would be considered a medical impossibility and a miracle from a religious standpoint* [italics are mine]. However I have watched the restoration year after year as I applied the power of thought, and I know it is under divine law. So I am satisfied that here is proof of a law that the mind builds the body and can restore it.[3]

Charles died at age 94, on July 5, 1948. Like Myrtle, he enjoyed health and vigor. He eventually walked with only a slight limp—a far cry from the crutches and four-inch extension.

What compelling testimony this is from both Charles and Myrtle Fillmore on how what we think and pray affects us.

In April 1889 Charles began publication of a magazine called *Modern Thought,* which a year later was renamed *Christian Science Thought* (although it, and the Fillmores, had no connection with the Christian Science church). Charles declared that the magazine would be devoted to "Pure Mind Healing," and he repudiated Spiritualism and occultism, which he said included such things as magnetism, hypnotism, mesmerism, psychometry, palmistry, and astrology. In 1891 the Fillmores changed the magazine's name again, to *Thought.* Then one night as they sat in prayer, Charles received the inspiration that it should be called *Unity.* The name stuck, and the Unity movement began to take shape.

The Fillmores spent much of the rest of their lives in constant prayer. One of their greatest legacies, the Silent Unity prayer service, is described in Chapter 11.

In their ministry, Myrtle Fillmore led people in prayer and meditation. Charles Fillmore did much writing and public speaking. Understandably, he had much to say about prayer and thought.

Prayer, he said, "awakens spiritual consciousness and develops true spiritual character. It is the only way to cleanse and perfect the mind and thus permanently heal the body. . . . True prayer brings about an exalted radiation of energy, and when it is accompanied by faith, judgment, and love, the word of Truth bursts forth in a stream of light that, when held in the mind, illumines, uplifts, and glorifies."[4] When the mind is lifted by prayer, he said, one's whole body glows with spiritual light.

He also said that the Holy Spirit in the Divine Mind (God), corresponds to thoughts in our mind. The ideas of the Divine Mind unfold through humanity.

> Mind is the storehouse of ideas. Man draws all his ideas from this omnipresent storehouse. The ideas of God, heaven, hell, devils, angels, and all things have their clue in Mind. But their form in the consciousness depends entirely upon the plane from which man draws his mental images. If he gets a "clue" to the character of God and then proceeds to clothe this clue with images from without, he makes God a mortal. If he looks within for the clothing of his clue idea, he knows God to be the omnipresent Spirit of existence.[5]

As for health and healing, Fillmore observed, "Thought makes the body and determines the condition it lives in. Thoughts of health are living, eternal things, and they work with the irresistible power of almightiness to tone up the organism to their own high state of harmony and capability."[6] Affirmations of any good statement of health put the human consciousness into contact with the Christ Mind, which releases energy stored in the subconscious that, when released, has a rejuvenating effect.

## Science of Mind

Not far behind the Fillmores in developing New Thought philosophy was Science of Mind, founded by Ernest Holmes. It, too, grew into a huge international movement.

Essentially, Science of Mind teaches that we are surrounded by an Infinite Intelligence, or Mind (God), which functions upon our beliefs. If we let go of destructive beliefs and replace them with constructive ones, we enter into a cooperation with this Mind that enables us to be healthier, happier, more successful and more spiritually fulfilled. To this end, daily affirmations, meditation, and prayer facilitate that objective.

Holmes taught that there is but one Mind and everything is an aspect of it; each of us uses a portion of It. He taught, "My thought is in control of my experience and I can direct my thinking," and "the ability to control my experiences and have them result in happiness, prosperity, and success lies in my own mind and my use of it."

"Mind responds to mind," said Holmes. "It is done to you as you believe." In other words, do not *ask* for things, but *declare* them. This is the Law of Mind, which manifests the beliefs we speak into It.

To improve health and for healing, Holmes recommended meditation upon affirmations such as "God-life surges through my entire body," or "I am well and successful in everything that I do," followed by a period of prayer in which the pray-er does not ask for anything, but declares desired results, accepts them as though they have manifested, and gives thanks for them. For example, one might declare, "I am prosperous because I believe in my prosperity. I accept the responsiveness of the Universe, and give thanks for my prosperity."

This method can be applied to any situation or need in life. One's thoughts and motives ideally should be God-like. A key element is belief in the desired results; Holmes stressed that belief must be felt with the total being. He noted that the effective prayer is one prayed by a person whose faith has removed all doubt.

## "Thoughts are things"

The New Thought movement may have brought the power of thought to new and more widespread attention, but the power of thought to influence physical reality—to literally create reality—is ancient wisdom. Esoteric philosophy holds that thoughts produce two effects: a radiating vibration and a floating, colored form, or thought-form, which exists in either the mental plane or astral plane. Thought-forms can be perceived by clairvoyants but may also be sensed on an intuitive level by others. Thought-forms attract sympathetic essences, thus forming the basis of the Law of Attraction, which holds that one attracts on the physical plane what one thinks on the mental plane.

Annie Besant and C. W. Leadbeater, both Theosophists and clairvoyants, said thought-forms fall into three classes: 1) the image of the thinker; 2) an image of a material object associated with the thought; and 3) an independent image expressing the inherent qualities of a thought. Thoughts that are low in nature, such as anger, hate, lust, greed, and so on, create thought-forms that are dense in color and form. Thoughts of a more spiritual nature generate forms that have greater purity, clarity, and refinement.

Thought-forms build up in a person's energy field or aura, creating and influencing behavior and characteristics. Negative thoughts weaken a person, even facilitating the onset of illness, while positive and loving thoughts act as a protective, energizing shield. According to Besant and Leadbeater, selfish thought moves in a curve, eventually coming back on itself (and the person) and expending itself on its own level. On the other hand, unselfish thought moves outward in an open curve, expanding as it goes. It is capable of piercing higher spiritual dimensions and thus becomes a channel through which higher planes pour themselves into lower planes. This is how prayer functions. Besant and Leadbeater stressed that regular meditation is important in cultivating positive thought-forms. The meditation sends out a stream of magnetism that continues to work long after the meditation is ended.

In describing thought-forms, Besant and Leadbeater noted that they are four-dimensional in nature, and therefore difficult to describe in three-dimensional terms. They said that well-sustained devotion could appear as a flower with upward curving petals like azure flames. Devotional aspiration might appear as a blue cone with the apex pointing upward to the higher planes. On the other side of the coin, explosive anger appears as a splash of red or orange, and sustained anger as a sharp, red stiletto. Jealousy might appear as a brown snake.

Their clairvoyance enabled them to see thought-forms created by a group effort, such as prayer. They affirmed that united thought is far more than the sum of the separate thoughts.

Norman Vincent Peale, who hailed from the different school of mainstream religion, also saw prayer as the sending out of vibrations, from one person to another and to God. In sending out a prayer, he said, we employ the force inherent in a spiritual universe and awaken vibrations through which God brings to pass the objectives prayed for.

## Prayerful thinking

"Prayer is a key to the source of power," said healer Ambrose Worrall. He appreciated the power of meditative and contemplative prayers and also prayers of petition and affirmation. However, one of the most important kinds of prayer is "prayer that is not usually considered a prayer," he said. That is thought. We pray merely by thinking.

"All our thoughts, all our conscious thinking, is in essence part of a prayer," he said. He elaborated:

> For as a man thinketh, so he is. Indeed, as he thinketh, so he prays.
> Millions of people, in many varieties of religions, pray—without thought, without purpose, reciting empty words that no longer have meaning to the one mouthing them because he does not listen to them himself, with his mind or heart or soul; he mumbles them with vague meaningless mumblings.

In mere thoughtlessness there can be no prayer. Yet the converse of this is also true: *Every thought is a prayer.*

In healing, the essence of the thought may achieve in an instant where a thousand verbalized entreaties fail. This is not because no one is listening, but because we, perhaps, ask amiss, because we are dealing not with whim but with universal law. . . .

Whether or not we go to church regularly, we still lead prayerful lives, though we may not know it. If we wish a man sick—it is a prayer, but a prayer for sickness, not good. If we think ill of him—it is a prayer, again of evil. If, in our mind, we see him in failure—it is a prayer for his failure. If we see him healthy, successful, if we think of him in terms of love, if we surround him and his family in our thoughts with love—this is prayer. Whatever we think about others, about ourselves, our world, becomes a prayer for or against others, for or against ourselves, for or against our world.[7]

Instead of asking, How should we pray? Worrall said, we should ask ourselves, How should we think? He advocated praying both silently and aloud, and the utilization of visualization.

In true prayer our thinking is an awareness that we are part of this Divine universe. Our thinking reaches out, it has power. Prayer is a dynamic sending out of a wish, a desire, a dream in the process of realization, a plan, a hope, a need, a striving. It may be, in fact, visualization, in picture form, of the condition desired. But it also must be imbued with the spirit of compassion and love of God.[8]

Worrall said that the "parrot-like repetition of phrases learned in various religious services" fails to reach the source of power and therefore lacks the dynamism to be effective. An effective prayer concentrates not on the elimination of a condition, but on the creation of a desired condition.

## Thought and health

In recent years, science has been able to demonstrate that what we think can strengthen or weaken our immune systems by triggering the production of certain chemicals that flood the body. For example, anger and rage stimulate the production of large amounts of epinephrine (adrenaline). Excessive amounts over a long period of time can raise blood pressure, which in turn contributes to heart disease, ulcers, and a host of other problems. Depression and self-doubt stimulate the production of hormones such as cortisone, which hampers the immune system.

Laboratory studies have demonstrated how thoughts affect the immune system. In one study conducted by the University of California at Los Angeles, actors performed both happy and sad scenes. Their immune systems were beneficially or adversely affected, respectively.

Two studies of joy and death showed how happy anticipation affected death rates. In one study, the death rate of Jewish men dropped significantly right before Passover, an important religious holiday. After Passover, the death rate increased above normal, then dropped to normal rates. Another study of elderly Chinese women showed similar results before, during, and after the Harvest Moon Festival, in which the symbolic importance of elderly women is recognized and honored.

Numerous other studies have shown similar results.

Our thought affects not only our own individual health, but the health of nations and, ultimately, our world. Meishu-sama, the Japanese founder of Johrei, observed:

> Prayer will suffice to solve any problem, for prayer is a form of communication with God. In earthly paradise, God's response will be direct and unambiguous, given the great depth of people's love for and understand-

ing of the divine, and the high degree to which their thoughts reflect that understanding.

Now, as in the past, we are given complete freedom in what we think. We may direct all our thoughts to God and to the great expanse of universe He created, or we may fill our hearts with petty desires, complaints, or evil thoughts. A person can think, wish, or feel in any way he chooses, *but his thoughts and feelings at any given time are automatically registered in the spiritual world* [italics are mine]. Sometimes they cause disturbing upsets and change in the realm of spirit, which . . . are eventually projected into the realm of matter. Thus, it is in the human heart that wars between nations, conflicts between individuals, and other forms of strife originate.

The freedom of will therefore carries with it moral responsibility for the consequences of all one's thoughts, words, and acts. God is aware of every single movement in our hearts and minds.[9]

In the next chapter, the power of prayer and the power of mind teach a doctor how to heal his own blindness.

# Six

# "Everyone Is Capable of a Miracle"

ai Kermani, M.D., is a general practitioner, stress-management consultant, counselor, healer, author, and poet who is well-known in England's health-care field. His credentials are long and impressive. Most notable—and the reasons I sought him out at his office/home in Essex, just outside of London—are his self-healing and his work with people with AIDS. Using meditative prayer and autogenics, a technique of deep relaxation, Dr. Kermani healed himself of total blindness. Using the same techniques, he has helped HIV-positive patients significantly raise the levels of their T-cells, which are crucial to the functioning of the body's immune system. T-cells help the body resist viral, bacterial, and fungal infections, as well as cancers. When the levels of T-cells in the body drop to dangerously low levels, the body becomes vulnerable to a host of invasions.

There are doctors, and then there are doctors who are healers. Kai Kermani falls into the latter category. He is not one of those physicians we find all too often in medical clinics: self-important, rushed and either disdainful of the patient's own intuitive body wisdom or too preoccupied to listen to what the patient has to say. Dr. Kermani believes in a holistic approach to health and illness, making use of the best of both conventional and alternative therapies whenever possible. He listens to the heard and unheard, and sees the seen and unseen.

Kermani has the traditional scientific education and training for a medical doctor. He began his career as a general practitioner. He is a member of most of the major Royal Medical Colleges. His own crisis of blindness led him into holistic health and alternative healing, as he describes in this chapter. It was through this crisis that his own healing gifts emerged.

In the mid-1980s, Kermani pioneered the concept of holistic management of HIV infection and AIDS in the U.K. Since then, he has worked with nearly one thousand HIV-positive and AIDS patients. Initially, he introduced autogenic training as the mainstay of stress management and self-healing. In recent years, he has used spiritual healing and simple meditation (a form of prayer) in place of autogenics, with good results. In his own spiritual healing work, he uses autogenics and meditative prayer. He also uses crystals, placing them over and under the bodywork table that patients lie on and also placing them on the body at various organ and chakra points.

Kermani is a member of the National Federation of Spiritual Healers, the British Holistic Medical Association, the Medical and Scientific Network, and the Doctor-Healer Network that Daniel J. Benor, M.D., helped to found. Kermani is the author of numerous articles and contributions to books. His own book, *Autogenic Training: The Effective Way to Conquer Stress,* has sold widely in the U.K. and abroad. He serves on the advisory boards of various health and medical journals and lectures internationally.

When I arrived at Dr. Kermani's office at home, I was greeted by a slender man whose gentle energy made me feel immediately at ease. Such is the case with healers. Through their accessing of divine energy for healing purposes, their own energy fields begin to glow as a result. Their work spaces, whether they be in an office, a home, or a religious site, also become imbued with the same residual energy.

I first asked Dr. Kermani to explain autogenic training.

Autogenic training, said Kai, as he preferred to be called, "is probably one of the most effective and powerful, yet simple techniques of relaxation that has been devised in the West. It was created in the 1930s in Germany. The name means 'self-generated'; 'autogen' literally means 'generated from within.' It was developed by a neuropsychologist who found that a sequence of things happens when people relax. It's a bit like when you fall asleep—you start feeling heavy and warm, for instance. He thought that concentration and these physical sensations could be utilized to bypass the conscious mind and access deeper levels of awareness.

"Autogenics consists of a series of simple mental exercises designed to turn off the stressful 'flight-or-fight' mechanism in the body and turn on the restorative and recuperative rhythms associated with profound psychophysical relaxation. If it is practiced daily, it brings results on the mental level comparable to those achieved by Eastern forms of meditation on the mental level, and on the physical level brings the chemical and physiological body changes associated with hard sports and physical training.

"It also enables people to get in touch with their deeper feelings of repressed emotions, and to deal with them effectively through specific exercises, so that the deep states of peace and tranquility which are achieved can be maintained on a prolonged basis."

Kai continued, "Autogenics is particularly appealing to the Western mind, because unlike many forms of meditation and yoga, it has no cultural, religious, or cosmological overtones, and requires no special clothing or unusual postures or positions. Perhaps most important, the physical and mental relaxation, as well as the feeling of peace and tranquility, are generated from within oneself and are not dependent on any external values, philosophies, or therapies. And, autogenics is a tool that can be used anywhere or anytime, unlike certain other forms of relaxation."

Kai explained that the exercises teach the trainee how to concentrate on normal physical sensations in order to achieve deep relaxation. "The focus of attention progresses from the limbs to the heart and circulation, the breathing and the nervous system, and thus to deep within oneself," he said. "The ability to do this, and achieve 'passive concentration' at will, breaks through the vicious cycle of excessive stress and tension, whatever the origins. The individual can use the technique anywhere or anytime in order to deal with a stressful situation or event."

Autogenics has been used to treat a wide range of maladies and also to improve performance in sports, business, education, and the creative arts.

I then asked Kai to talk about his blindness and how he healed himself.

"About fourteen years ago, I discovered that I was suffering from an untreatable medical condition which would lead me to total blindness," he began. "It is called retinitis pigmentosa. It is a disease that leads to the progressive destruction of the retina, and there is nothing you can do to stop it, according to convention.

"True to the prognosis, I went blind in my right eye, and then the left one began following suit. So, I decided to learn something else that I could do to earn a living when I did go blind.

"That's when I got involved with psychotherapy, because I thought I would not need my vision to practice that. I heard about autogenics— all sorts of claims were being made as to what it does. Being a scientist before I became a doctor, I was exceedingly skeptical. I thought, well, the proof of the pudding is in the eating. So I tried it. That opened my mind. I became very interested in psychoneuro-immunology and the power of the mind. Now, if we have the power to make ourselves sick, or contribute to our illnesses, then we also have the power to heal ourselves. That would apply to my blindness. I undoubtedly had the power within me to make myself better.

"Using autogenics, I reversed the partial blindness in the left eye, and the vision returned to complete normality, which I enjoyed for some years. In May 1991, unfortunately, I had an accident. Two builders had put some sharp objects out, which I didn't see. I bent down to put a milk bottle out and pierced my good eyeball. I was completely blinded, because I lost the front of the eye, and the contents of it. The medical consultant who had looked after me for years said, 'There's no way you can get any sight back because you've mechanically lost the eye this time.'

"I didn't think much of that verdict. I had surgery to reconstruct as much of the eyeball as possible. I started working again on regaining my vision, three to four hours a day. My visual acuity now has come back to complete normality, although I still have some restriction because of the mechanical gadgets that I have to wear. I'm wearing a specially constructed lens to obstruct the incoming light because, having lost the iris, too much light would otherwise get in. I live on my own. I carry on with all my writing and lectures and all the rest of it.

"I also started working on my right eye, which had gone blind from the disease. I've got some vision back in it now. The central portion is still totally blind, but I have some peripheral vision. I'm working on it, and I'm determined for it to be normal."

"Essentially, you've delivered a miracle to yourself," I said.

"Well, yes, but it is something that everybody is capable of doing," Kai said with modesty. "I got in touch with that power through autogenic training, which is just one way of doing it. I've also used prayer, done in a meditative way. The meditative prayer is very, very important. Ordinary prayer, like prayer in church, doesn't work the same, in my opinion. You've got to spend time and concentrate in order to get in touch with that deep power within you. Prayers done in a prolonged, meditative way do work and enable you to get in touch with that power. Praying for others will work, too, even in distant healing.

"About two or three years before the accident, I became aware that I had the gift of healing. Despite my involvement with complementary therapies, that struck me as weird stuff—after all, I was a general practitioner, and I came out of a science background. People started commenting on this gift while I was still in general practice. Patients came to me and said things like their frozen shoulder would clear up after me having examined them. They could feel energy coming out of me. One man said, 'Look, you're a healer.'

"It took me a long time to develop it. Like most healers, I started doing healing on friends and family initially. I used autogenics to connect to the energy. It takes me a couple of minutes to completely center myself. Then I connect, and I become part of the energy, which I see as a path of golden light. I, the healee, and the light all become one. Then I'm able to move energy about. When I first started doing this, I would see a vision when I got into that state.

"Originally, I was a Zoroastrian by faith. Zoroastrianism is the most ancient religion in Iran, preceding Islam. It's the oldest religion that believed in one God, with Zoroaster as his prophet. It's about 4,000 to 6,000 years old. My current philosophy for a rich, contented life is loosely based on this ancient wisdom. Briefly, it advocates good, pure positive thoughts; good, loving and encouraging words; good, helpful and unconditional deeds and actions; and finally, good, clear, peaceful and uplifting vision for ourselves, those around us, and the world.

"When I did healing on other people, I would see this image of an enormous well above me. On one side was Zoroaster, and on the other side was Christ on the cross. When I started the healing, divine light would come through the Zoroaster aspect, but the Christ aspect was dark. It was unpleasant, because I could see Christ suffering, but I couldn't get him off the cross in this vision.

"After the surgery on my injured eye, I did autogenics, and a message came through to me, 'You must start healing again now.' I thought, 'Well, that's a fat lot of good! I'm lying here blind and this is a bit much!

"But I did start healing, within a month. I still couldn't see. It was interesting that in the first healing that I did after the surgery, I had the vision and this time Christ was off the cross. He was wearing a white robe, and the light was coming through both him and Zoroaster, which took me completely by surprise. That went on for months. Then gradually that image disappeared, and then I just saw one cross of light. Now I just see intense light—in fact, I become part of this intense light.

"I have been using autogenics since 1984 with people who are HIV-positive. People who've had advanced AIDS also have come to me. Back in the early 1980s, they didn't even know how to treat their pneumonias, let alone any other complications from AIDS. With autogenics and a holistic approach that includes diet and nutritional supplements, people found that no matter how ill they were, they started improving after seeing me. They controlled their symptoms. They were able to improve their quality of life, which was the most important thing. And as a result, a great many of them prolonged their lives quite considerably. About forty percent of them survived five years. Considering that this was in the early 1980s, that was a very good prognosis!

"Then my own partner, Edward, died from AIDS, just as I was getting my vision back, which was devastating. This was a particularly bitter blow, as he had lived healthily with the condition for five years, using the techniques that I advocate. His T-cells at the time of diagnosis were under fifty! His only serious infection was misdiagnosed and was, in my opinion, not treated as it should have been. I believe this is what killed him, and not his original condition.

"I was so depressed that I stopped working with patients, including people who were HIV. I stopped doing anything because I felt at the time that I could not give anything to anyone.

"Then, people started coming back to me. It is interesting that this only happened after I worked through my grief and bereavement—almost as if the 'management upstairs' had organized the time that I was ready to see patients again! But this time, they were not those who had advanced AIDS, but HIV-positive people who were asymptomatic. They came because their T-cell levels were dropping consistently. The normal range for T-cells is between five hundred to fifteen hundred, and the average is about one thousand. When the level drops below two hundred, they may start having serious complications and infections.

"Recently I gave four patients eight sessions each. I've found about six to eight sessions seems to be about what most people need for most conditions. But those with serious or chronic conditions seem to need a few 'top up' sessions every three to four months. Some of the first session was devoted to the taking of the patient's history and discussion of their health habits and how they can be improved. I recommended various vitamins and trace elements, and also advised them to take hyssop tea infusions, because this Biblically known herb is believed to have some antiviral properties. I also recommended lecithin forte, because it is believed to alter the outer fatty layer of the cells and thus interfere with the ability of the AIDS virus to penetrate and reinfect new cells. This is then followed by healing.

"The early part of the second session was devoted to counseling, and the latter part to healing, which lasted about an hour. Typically, I had the person lie flat on a massage table. I first worked on the back with the energy lines and minor chakras in the limbs. Normally, I work through the auric fields, so I rarely touch anyone, unless it feels intuitively appropriate to do so.

"On the front side, I worked on all the major and minor chakras, concentrating particularly on the thymus gland, between the heart and throat chakras, and the main lymph glands in the armpits and groins. It is the thymus gland that gives its name to the T-cells—the *T* stands for thymus.

"As for the crystals, I intuitively select the ones to use based on deficiencies that I pick up in the auras. However, I consistently use a clear generator quartz crystal on the crown chakra, an amethyst cluster directed to the third-eye chakra, a blue agate and large turquoise stone on the thymus, a rose quartz on the heart chakra, malachite and citrine on the solar plexus chakra, turquoise and-or chrysocolla over major lymph glands, such as in the armpits and on the groins. I also use obsidian on the groins and near the root chakra.

"After about eight sessions of healing, every single one of them had their T-cells increase by almost fifty percent—that was an *enormous* increase. Counts went from 190 to 310, 190 to 280, 300 to 480 and 450 to 620. I've had one person since then whose T-cells haven't gone up but have remained static, and he has stabilized for the first time in a long time. The client whose T-cells went from 300 to 480 experienced another increase to 520 after a second round of six sessions of healing. This was despite the stress of a disastrous breakup of his long-standing relationship. He has since acknowledged his own healing powers and is training to become a complementary therapist.

"None of these patients are using any conventional therapy. They didn't want to go on antibiotics, AZT, or other drugs. That's why they started coming to me. Most of them are determined with positive attitudes that they can beat AIDS. I advise a holistic approach—diet, nutritional supplements, looking after themselves."

"Why has autogenics been so effective with the HIV patients?" I asked.

"The quick answer is because it gives them an effective tool to fight the condition with," Kai said. "This empowerment stops them from feeling like hopeless and helpless victims. However, the mechanics with which it does that are a bit more complicated. I teach autogenics in eight-week sessions in small groups, because group interaction enables people to learn from each other. It can be done individually, as well.

"First they learn to concentrate on their normal physical sensations—heaviness, warmth, and so on. Then we begin to work inward. As you know, we repress a lot of emotions into different levels of our physical body, emotional body, and mental body.

"So we work gradually inwards to the heart, circulation, breathing, and then to the solar plexus. The solar plexus is the junction box of the so-called autonomic nervous system. We concentrate on this area because it's also the seat of the emotions and the intuition. It is then possible to get in touch with emotional stuff that needs to be off-loaded. I teach exercises on how to off-load.

"Once emotional knots are cleared from the solar plexus, they can start controlling the autonomic nervous system, which enables them to indirectly affect the functions of the brain. These include the chemicals that are released by the brain, such as hormones. Thus, they can influence their entire hormonal system as well as their neuroendocrine system.

"Effects include a drop in blood pressure and cholesterol. If they can control or influence these, then it is possible for them to influence the levels of their T-cells or control their HIV symptoms.

"When healing is done, people get very relaxed. This affects their autonomic nervous system, particularly the solar plexus region. Part of this whole process is empowering people to look after themselves. That's exceedingly important. The way I think about it, it is like the pilot light to the boiler of their central heating system. Once lighting it happens, then they go on firing on their own. This is the beginning of the very important self-empowerment process. Often people only need two or three sessions to clear something up, like a back problem."

"You mentioned the importance of meditative prayer," I said. "Could you explain how that differs from other kinds of prayer?"

Kai replied, "There are two points about meditative prayer. Most of the prayers that people do puts the power 'out there.' They expect God or Christ or Allah or Buddha or whoever, to do it for them. They totally disempower themselves by putting all of the power out there: '*You* change this. *You* make me better. *You* heal me.' Whereas in meditative prayer, the person takes responsibility for him- or herself, and as a consequence gets in touch with the God within, the power within, the strength within, and the light and unconditional love within.

"Now you do need the help from without too. God or the divine power, or whatever you like to call it, controls our energy systems because we're part of it. We need to get in touch with it deep within us. Then we have to use that power to overcome our problem. To me, the true healer, the true miracle worker, is myself—the person I see in the mirror.

"Another thing about the way most people pray: just spending a couple of minutes at it, doesn't work—like kids who sit by their bedside and put their hands together and say, 'God protect Mom and Dad.' You really need to spend time, at least twenty minutes, in total quiet and stillness. This is the time when the power and strength of God within can get connected to, and greatly enhanced by, the power of the God without. It is also during this quiet period that the true communication between you and the Divine Power can take place, and you can hear his quiet voice of truth and wisdom. You need to become totally at one not only with the space of love and healing within you but also with the space of love and healing without you. It's an intensely deep experience. You can work on yourself or you can send healing prayers to others at a distance.

"Initially, to enter into that state, I used autogenics. Now I use a combination of things, depending on what feels appropriate at the time and whether I'm sending distant healing. I spend a minimum of an hour at least once a day in this meditative prayer. I also do shorter periods of ten or fifteen minutes, during the day, and then again as my last thing at night before I go to bed. This is also the time when I send healing to the spirits of those who have died, especially those who have died with disease or distress. Although healing energy is mediated by the highly evolved spirits, those who are still going through their process of evolution and development, especially our loved ones who have passed on, need our healing prayers. Furthermore, although the spirit world—and especially the spirits of our nearest and dearest who have passed on—are longing to help us on the earth plane, they cannot do it of their own volition. We have to give them permission, and ask for their help in our prayers and meditations.''

Kai cautioned that while we can connect to God in the quiet, we can also connect to the "demons and dark shadows that lurk in the recesses of our minds. Actually, this is a wonderful opportunity to get to know and let go of them and consequently bring more light and love into our lives. Perhaps this is a reason why so many people feel uncomfortable and uneasy being quiet. It might also explain why there is hardly ever any significant period of silence and contemplation during most conventional church services.''

Kai said that he is conservative about using the word 'prayer' with new patients, because prayer is so intimately linked with organized religion, and many people have sensitivities about religion. "I talk about energy transfer instead," he said. "I start them with a very simple meditation that is in fact a deep form of prayer. I tell them to imagine energy coming up from the earth through them and changing color. I go through the rainbow colors of the chakras—red, orange, yellow, green, and so on. The colors change to white, and then I ask them to imagine an enormous white source of light above them, and to bring that down into them. To some, that big white source up there is God or Christ. To others, it is a nameless universal energy. However they think of it, they can still connect with it, and use it.

"As long as most people think of this as energy transfer rather than prayer—even though it's really a form of prayer—they're fine. But you say 'prayer' and sometimes a whole lot of religious beliefs kick in. Many people who go to church are fixed in their ways about things such as prayer, belief systems and the existence of alternative realities and different ways of attaining spiritual awareness and enlightment. This fixedness can be an obstruction to healing, particularly in HIV, where the conflict between sexuality and religious dogma can be very strong and unproductive. The suggestion of change may be almost abhorrent to many who have rigid belief systems. In my experience this seems to apply particularly in traditions like Catholicism and high Protestantism. However, I do not wish to sound as if I am decrying or demeaning the importance of conventional, organized religion, as that could be the only way through which a great many people find their spirituality. But in order for these individuals to nurture and allow their spirituality to bloom fully, they must be flexible and open to change and transformation, whether it be through the medium of autogenics, meditation or prayer. It is only then that the individual can truly connect with the spirit and light of God.

"I'm eclectic in my views and I've attended various churches. I don't call myself religious at all, actually. I call myself highly spiritual. I feel just as happy praying in anybody's temple or church or mosque. I strongly believe that true spiritual awareness transcends the confines of religious dogma.

"Science also puts blinkers on us. When I was a conventional general practitioner, nobody could have been more blinkered or fixed in their views than I was. I'd been brought up as a scientist, and it was only when I started having my own health problems that I started opening my mind. I never used to think about my own healing powers, let alone those of the patient consulting me! Now I realize that the only limitations to healing are the ones we set for ourselves. Healing is unlimited.

"For instance, if you cut yourself, you never think that it's not going to heal, do you? You just stick a bandage on it and just let go—it's settled! But if somebody tells you you've got a growth, you say, 'Oh, there's no way I can heal that!' But why? What's different about that? It is just what we've been *told*! Your horizon is limited to healing your little wounds. When a surgeon cuts you open, who or what is it that heals the ten or twelve layers of tissue, muscles, and skin? It's not the surgeon. He just cobbles you up with stitches. It's the inner wisdom of the body that does the healing! But we don't think about that."

"We've given away our power to heal," I commented.

"Absolutely! We've disempowered ourselves. I'm delighted when patients don't have to see me again, because I know they're doing their own work." Kai shook his head. "I realize now how blinkered I was as a general practitioner. I was an extremely good technical doctor. But I used to think that it was genuinely me and my pills and potions that actually cured people! Now I realize that it is the individual who cures himself, with a little help from me.

"That doesn't mean conventional medicine and doctors aren't necessary. We need a combination of help. For instance, there was no way that my natural healing abilities could have pulled all the shattered bits of my eyeball together. I needed a surgeon to do that. But he only did the technical part—the final healing came from within me."

I asked Kai what other illnesses or disorders besides AIDS and cancer he's worked with as a spiritual healer. Several patients with advanced multiple sclerosis succeeded in clearing up their symptoms. A woman—a general practitioner who was skeptical about alternative healing—came suffering from chronic fatigue syndrome and had a complete reversal.

A priest whose bad back kept him confined to bed was able after two sessions to get up and resume preaching. He was so impressed that he started healing services in his church, said Kai.

Another patient was a man with three prolapsed disks, which were pressing on his sciatic nerve, and who could barely walk when he came to see Kai. He had been advised to have surgery right away. He was reluctant to do so, and even though he was skeptical about healing, he decided to give it a try. He arrived for his first session on crutches, dragging one leg behind him. After the third session, his symptoms were completely cleared up. He was able to swim, drive, garden, and get about. His medical consultant told him he should have been paralyzed. Three years later, he still is problem-free.

"How can prayer influence our overall wellness?" I asked.

"I genuinely believe that if we all work sufficiently on ourselves to clear our channels and thus get in touch with our healing powers, through prayer and meditation, humanity could become incredibly healthy and peaceful. This in turn could create heaven on earth instead of the current mess and chaos. I really believe that. I think we are going toward that goal. People are becoming much, much more aware. The energy level of consciousness is rising throughout the world. I believe by the year 2000 or soon thereafter, the energy level will reach a critical point that everybody suddenly will become aware."

Kai offered to give me a demonstration of a healing. I quickly agreed. I am a firm believer in energy healing, having benefited from it as a patient and also having seen its tangible force as a student of various spiritual transfer techniques.

He took me into a small healing sanctuary with a pleasant atmosphere of plants and crystals. There were myriads of crystals, hanging over the bodywork table, resting under the table, and placed neatly on a side table. Kai explained that crystals facilitate the movement of healing energy. He selects the kinds and shapes of crystals according to the health problem at hand or according to his intuitive guidance.

I asked him if he was aware of angelic guides. He said he knew they were always present, but had never seen any. Some of his patients sense and see them. His deceased partner, Edward, sometimes appears as a helping presence, as well.

I lay down on the bodywork table and relaxed. Kai asked if I had any health problems or would like just a general healing. Since our available time was restricted, he could give only a short sample healing.

I had only two health problems, I explained: an ovarian cyst that had been present for some years, and pain in one knee, the cause of which I did not know.

Kai selected some crystals and placed them at specific chakra points on my body. As he centered himself in meditative prayer, I closed my eyes and also prayed. I descended into a state of deep relaxation—so deep that I fell asleep. Falling asleep is common in healing and bodywork, but I had never felt so profoundly relaxed as I did that afternoon in Kai's studio.

It seemed as if I slept for a long time, but in fact I was really "out" for only about ten minutes, Kai said. I drifted up and down on pleasant waves of hypnagogic sleep that were filled with images.

Kai said that when sleep happens, he can clairvoyantly see the spirit leave the body. It is during that time, he believes, that the healing takes place—when one is sort of vacated and out of the way.

I felt energized and refreshed upon arising.

Kai said the pain in my knee was due to an inflammation under the kneecap. Later, after I returned to the States, I went to an orthopedist to get another diagnosis. It was exactly the same. As for my cyst, as I explained in the introduction, it was gone about two weeks later.

Thus far, we have seen prayer at work in a variety of situations. For Ann Marie in Chapter 1, healing came with prayer of surrender. Guy Riggs in Chapter 3 and Kai Kermani used directed, active prayer. And the researchers in Chapter 4 successfully used both directed and nondirected (surrender) prayer. Are these experiences contradictory? What do they tell us about the "right" ways to pray?

# Seven

# THE ART OF SUCCESSFUL PRAYER

When we ask for something in prayer and then receive it, we can only marvel at the awesome power prayer unleashes. Answered prayers make us feel blessed and lucky. Prayer seems to be a useful tool to getting what we want in the world. Norman Vincent Peale, the minister who became famous for advocating positive thinking, termed prayer "the most tremendous power in the world."

Yet, we've all had prayers that seem to go unanswered, and we wonder why. Did we not approach the matter properly? Did we not say the right words? Did God turn a deaf ear to us? Was what we asked for not right for us? Is there anything we can do to improve our success in prayer?

These questions are often hard to answer. Every situation involving prayer is complex, with many subtle factors at work. Prayer involves more than a collection of words, thoughts, and intents. For example, we may be undergoing certain trials in order to learn lessons on a soul level. Consequently, if we pray for deliverance or relief, we may not get quite what we expect.

## Are prayers always answered?

The apostle James said that prayers that seem to be unanswered mean that "ye ask amiss"; in other words, one is not asking for what is right or with sufficient belief and faith. Charles Fillmore, the cofounder of Unity, said that faith acts like electricity, which speeds the answers to prayers. If no answer is forthcoming, that means a lack of "proper mental adjustment of the mind" on the part of the pray-er.

However, no answer is still an answer; thus, prayers are *always* answered. Sometimes the answer is not the one we want to hear. Sometimes the answer is "no" to what we ask. As we saw earlier, Ann Marie Davis, extremely ill with cancer and Legionnaires' disease, prayed to die. The answer was no. Likewise, Maurice Williams, seriously ill with kidney failure, also prayed to die (Chapter 9). Sue (Chapter 12), who endured decades of abuse and addiction, was often shocked at how her prayers were answered. In Chapter 8 is the story of how Unity minister and executive Chris Jackson dealt with the unwanted answer to his prayer.

It's difficult to accept what we don't want to hear. This is particularly poignant in cases of life-threatening illness, in which people die despite the earnest prayers of many to the contrary.

"Prayer is not like turning on the oven," observes Daniel J. Benor, M.D. "We ask in prayer because we are not in control. Maybe we want a quick fix—we want God to solve our problem, when we need to be doing the work ourselves.

"The reason for illness may be beyond our immediate comprehension. We may have lessons to learn through the illness or other problems. Part of our lesson may be with people who are close to us. Maybe we have not learned to ask for help from those around us. Part of healing may be releasing old hurts.

"Some cancer patients believe that they allowed cancer to develop because their life situations, either personal or professional, were intolerable. They didn't see a way out. It can take a long time to get to those awarenesses behind the illness."[1]

"The prayer that is answered is your life prayer," says Mary-Alice Jafolla, who, with her husband, Richard Jafolla, codirects Silent Unity, the prayer ministry of the Unity School of Christianity. "Your life prayer is what you think and say all day long. Many people ask and beg during prayer time. The rest of the time they're living contrary to their prayers. Then they wonder why their prayers do not appear to be answered. But prayers—the prayers of our hearts—are always answered."[2]

Mary-Alice Jafolla cites as an example a man she and her husband Richard once knew. He suffered from lung cancer and devoted fifteen minutes twice a day to prayer, earnestly affirming healthy lungs. But did he live his prayer? No. The rest of the time, he continued to smoke. In fact, he smoked right up until the day before he died, cursing God for not answering his prayers.

That may seem like an extreme example, but all of us can probably think of ways we negate our prayers by not fully living them. If we can give ourselves an honest self-assessment, we can improve our life prayer immeasurably.

"If your thoughts, feelings, and actions agree with your formal prayers, then you have access to great power and can expect seeming miracles," says Mary-Alice. "You can't expect a ten-dollar answer from a ten-cent prayer. You've got to live your prayer with a God-filled life." As for miracles, Mary-Alice and Richard Jafolla do not consider them to be outside of cosmic law. That's why they call them "seeming miracles." Miracles may be things beyond our expectations, but they are still within the natural outworking of God's law. Believing that you need a miracle in order to fix a problem or be healed, in fact, limits the power of prayer, they say. "By focusing too specifically, we ignore the fact that God's desire for us is total good," says Mary-Alice. "We don't need miracles to bring that good to us. God's very nature is one of wholeness, abundance, and love. We are part of God's creation, and so we inherit all of that."[3]

Prayers are always answered, but the answers are never just for one person, states Unity minister and mystic Jim Rosemergy (who is profiled in Chapter 13). "Answered prayer is a consciousness of God which becomes Spirit's avenue into the world. Spirit now has eyes to see, ears to hear, a voice with which to speak, hands with which to touch, and a mind and heart with which to pour the blessings of the kingdom upon humankind. Answered prayer is not only for the one; it is for the many."[4]

## Synchronicity

One way that prayers are answered seems indirect but does have a direct impact on our lives. That is through synchronicity. Carl G. Jung termed synchronicity "an acausal connecting principle" that links seemingly unrelated and unconnected events—that is, coincidences, which are popularly discounted as chance happenings. In fact, there seems to be an invisible cause-and-effect relationship involving synchronicities, one which is governed by states of consciousness.

The concept of synchronicity was developed largely by Jung, who credited Albert Einstein as his inspiration. He was also influenced by the Viennese physicist Wolfgang Pauli. Jung was intrigued by "coincidences" that seemed far beyond the realm of probability. For example, he cited incidents that happened to the wife of a patient: upon the deaths of her mother and grandmother, birds gathered outside the windows of the death chamber. Jung noted the connection of birds to the soul or to messengers of the gods in various mythologies.

Jung, who first used the term "synchronicity" in 1930, also equated synchronicity with the Tao, the seamless flux and flow of the cosmos. He said synchronicity can be found in events that are meaningfully but not causally related (that is, do not coincide in time and space), as well as in events that do coincide in time and space and have meaningful psychological connections. In addition, synchronicity links the material world to the psychic; synchronistic events, he said, "rest on an archetypal foundation."

Many people who pray or meditate regularly find that synchronicities increase in their lives. It is as though they achieve a certain attunement with the universe, and it speaks back to them in the form of meaningful coincidences. Mystics in the East have been aware of this phenomenon for at least 2,500 years. The Upanishads state, "When the mind rests steady and pure, then whatever you desire, those desires are fulfilled."

A widespread increase in synchronicity would be indicative of a collective shift in consciousness toward higher levels, as we will see in Chapter 14.

## Answers in past lives

The concept of reincarnation may play a role in how prayers are answered. According to various opinion polls, an increasing number of Westerners—up to twenty-five percent of the adult population—either believe in reincarnation or are at least open to the idea.

Says Daniel J. Benor, M.D., "If we start asking about why things happen, we may have to look to previous lives. Some of the reasons why prayers appear not to be answered may have to do with lessons we have chosen in this life. Even though we might not be happy with having an illness, some part of our higher self may have chosen that illness as an important illness in this life. We may have been cruel or insensitive in a previous life to others' suffering, so we may have to suffer in order to grow and understand that part of ourselves.

"We don't have the ability to understand the true nature of reincarnation. Some aspect of ourselves survives death. I don't know exactly what that is. But there is an awareness that seems to persist from life to life, and our lessons seem to resonate backward as well as forward. The lessons I am learning now may have an effect on previous lives as well as on future lives."[5]

## Is there a right way to pray?

Benor echoes the views of many experts on prayer with this observation: "The ways to pray are as many and varied as there are individuals."

"Prayer," says Silent Unity co-director Richard Jafolla, "is simply speaking to God, aloud or silently, in whatever manner feels comfortable. What's more important than the method of praying is the *reason* for praying. Prayers are not to impress God. They are to impress us. They raise us to the level of consciousness where we can realize that we are one with God and therefore every good for us already exists."[6]

Indeed, there is no one "right" way to pray. How you pray depends upon your need, your prayer habits, your religious background, if any, and your spiritual beliefs. Religious background and spiritual beliefs are not necessarily the same. Spiritual experiences often expand upon, or even conflict with, traditional religious beliefs, thus changing the way we pray.

There *are* times when learned religious prayers are very appropriate to meet a need. The repeating of something familiar and tried-and-true over ages brings a certain comfort and reassurance. In Christianity, the Lord's Prayer, also called the Paternoster, is probably the most-repeated prayer. It also possesses incredible transformative power, according to minister Jim Rosemergy. Words spoken in prayer are "a manifestation of a soul in union with God," says Rosemergy.

"The Lord's Prayer gives us a rare glimpse of the consciousness or interior life of one who is one with Spirit. This precious gift Jesus gave to us is like the trellis that supports the growth of a climbing rosebush. The Lord's Prayer is the trellis upon which our spiritual life can grow and blossom. It is a blueprint founded upon Truth that outlines the structure of our interior life. The statements that make up the prayer are principles of life."[7]

The Lord's Prayer is:

> Our Father, who art in heaven,
> Hallowed be thy name,
> Thy kingdom come,
> Thy will be done,
> On earth as it is in heaven.
> Give us this day our daily bread.
> And forgive us our debts,
> As we forgive our debtors.
> And lead us not into temptation,
> But deliver us from evil.
> For thine is the kingdom and the power and the glory,
> Forever and ever.
> Amen.

Millions of people around the world do not consider their day complete, or their church service complete, without saying the Lord's Prayer. Another oft-repeated prayer is the Twenty-third Psalm, which imparts soothing, healing feelings.

The Twenty-third Psalm is:

> The Lord is my shepherd,
> I shall not want;
> He maketh me to lie down in green pastures.
> He leadeth me beside still waters;

He restoreth my soul.
He leadeth me in the paths of righteousness
For his name's sake.
Yea, though I walk through the valley
Of the shadow of death,
I fear no evil;
For thou art with me;
Thy rod and thy staff,
They comfort me.
Thou preparest a table before me
In the presence of my enemies.
Thou anointest my head with oil;
My cup runneth over.
Surely goodness and mercy shall follow me
All the days of my life,
And I shall dwell in the house of the Lord
Forever.

There are times when spontaneous prayer is more appropriate than learned, formal prayers. And, there are different times for thanksgiving, adoration, petition, intercession, and surrender. Let your intuition be your guide. Pray what you feel in your heart.

"Prayer is talking to God," says Richard Jafolla. "It is a communication from your individual mind to the Universal Mind of God. You can talk about anything you want. But the highest use of prayer is to announce your intention of opening yourself to God's will and God's good. In prayer, we invite God to be lived through us—we ask for and accept all of the qualities of God."[8]

Ultimately, the way to learn how to pray successfully is to do it. "We need to practice prayer in order to experience it," says Benor. "I can tell you about the taste of a cactus, but you won't actually know until you taste it yourself. By praying and doing it, we open ourselves to other realms. There's no right way or wrong way—just the way that's right for each person."[9]

Some researchers, however, believe that there *are* things that can tip the scales in favor of successful prayer.

## Parker's key to successful prayer

Several decades ago, Dr. William R. ("Cherry") Parker, an American college professor, psychologist, and speech pathologist, became interested in prayer and how people pray. Beginning in 1951, he conducted experiments in a university setting and published his results in a best-selling book, *Prayer Can Change Your Life* (1957), written with Elaine St. Johns.

"Prayer can change your life anytime, anywhere, at any age," asserted Parker. "It can heal your diseases, renew your mind and body, calm the storms of daily living from the great tempests of fear and sorrow that threaten to overwhelm—to the day by day squall in human relationships that constantly rock our boat until we view a world distorted by a seasick haze."[10]

This is not a "Valentine philosophy," Parker went on. He had proved through his own experience, and his experiments, that prayer works.

Parker screened forty-five volunteers and divided them into three groups of fifteen each. All volunteers had compelling health and/or relationship problems. Group I was Psychotherapy. These people received psychological counseling every week without mention of religion. Group II was Random Pray-ers. These persons had been schooled in a theological denomination and were devout, practicing Christians. All believed firmly in the power of prayer and felt that they knew how to pray. For the nine-month experiment, they agreed to pray every night before going to bed. They were not given any psychological counseling, nor were they given any suggestions on how to pray. Group III was Prayer Therapy. This group was conducted like a class investigating all aspects of prayer. They also received psychological counseling. The groups had no communication with each other.

At the end of the nine months, many people had experienced either improvement in their conditions or total relief. In some cases, there were dramatic physical healings attributed to prayer. Stuttering, arthritis, migraine headache, and high blood pressure responded to the power of prayer. A professor forced to retire because of tuberculosis regained his health and returned to teaching. A woman who continued to suffer epileptic seizures despite surgery to relieve a pressure point in her brain found complete relief through prayer. Marital problems, low self-esteem, and nervous disorders also cleared up.

In Group I, those who received psychotherapy only, there was a sixty-five percent improvement. In Group II, those who prayed nightly without psychological counseling, there was no improvement, even some backsliding in some cases. In Group III, Prayer Therapy, there was a remarkable seventy-two percent improvement.

Parker concluded that Prayer Therapy "was not only a most effective healing agent but that prayer properly understood might be the single most important tool in the reconstruction of man's personality. . . . Further, results indicated that Prayer Therapy provided something additional to psychology, supplied something that was missing to complete the healing process."[11]

But prayer plus psychotherapy was not the complete picture. Parker said the success of prayer depends on how we pray.

The key to successful prayer is remarkably simple. It is honesty. Total honesty.

"We must look honestly within," said Parker. "Until we do, we have little insight into what drives us, or why; in other words, no conscious control over our decisions and actions. Our outward selves will be automatons following deeply hidden unconscious patterns and we will in no ways be that entity with free will and self-choice in which we all believe."[12]

Parker believed that many people "pray amiss," which is why, as the apostle James said, their prayers do not seem to work. He opined that the Random Pray-ers in Group II evidently suffered this problem. He identified four "demons" that interfere with the power of prayer: fear, feelings of inferiority, guilt, and hate. They contribute to negative prayers, which in turn yield negative results. By being honest with ourselves, we can identify and confront the inner demons, and make improvements.

*Fear.* Parker observed that fear is the motivating power behind all repressions and suppressions. Fear limits and binds us and prevents us from reaching our full potential. He cited seven of the most common fears.

1. Fear of failure. Feelings of inadequacy defeat us before we begin.
2. Fear of sexual misunderstanding. This contributes to mistrust, frigidity, selfishness, and inability to form deep relationships.
3. Fear of defenselessness. A failure to defend one's own rights leads to all manner of infringements, often resulting in stress-related illness.
4. Fear of trusting others. Not being able to trust or depend upon others leads to isolation.
5. Fearful thinking. If we don't understand and accept that our thoughts affect our outer world, we give negative thinking too much power.
6. Fear of speaking. The inability to speak what is on our mind makes us dependent, suggestible, and submissive.
7. Fear of being alone. If we are restless and constantly seek diversion in order to avoid spending time with ourselves, we miss opportunities for insight, inner growth, creativity, inspiration, and communion with God.

*Feelings of Inferiority.* Low self-esteem contributes to excessive sensitivity and self-consciousness and to withdrawal or, at the opposite extreme, superiority complexes.

*Guilt.* Many people pray guilt-riddled prayers, thanks largely to religious indoctrination that teaches us that we're all miserable, worthless sinners until we are saved. The burden of original sin, taught by the Catholic Church, is particularly onerous. Many people spend their lives trying to put their spiritual house in order, hopelessly handicapped from the outset by negative conditioning. They prostrate themselves before God, apologizing for being unworthy.

No wonder such prayers don't achieve desired results, said Parker. Feelings of unworthiness and self-condemnation—which are not the same as humility and true confession—serve only to offer up to the subconscious a steady diet of negative reinforcement. As we learned in Chapter 5, thoughts are things and create our reality. Negative thoughts create negative conditions, compounding our difficulties.

Rather, we should approach prayer from the position that we are worthy to receive the blessings we seek. And, we should follow the advice given by Jesus and believe that we have already received those blessings. Before we utter so much as a word or think a thought, we must already have chosen health instead of illness, success instead of failure, peace and harmony instead of discord, etc.

*Hate.* Fear, guilt, and inferiority feelings involve our concept of love, said Parker. Hate is misguided love. "There are only three ways to feel toward another person," he said. "We can love them, hate them, or be indifferent toward them. What hate and indifference do to us mentally, physically, and spiritually is to keep us partially whole, sick, or dying."[13]

## The golden key

According to minister Emmet Fox, the "golden key" to successful prayer is, like Parker's honesty, a simple formula: "Stop thinking about the difficulty, whatever it is, and think about God instead." This, says Fox, is scientific prayer that "will enable you to get yourself, or anyone else, out of any difficulty."

The golden key enables the pray-er to get out of the way and become a divine channel through which God works. The pray-er's limitations, weaknesses, and expectations do not cloud the picture.

Fox advises that the pray-er not anticipate any particular solution. He calls this "outlining" and says it slows down results. Nor should the pray-er try to think about God by forming a picture of God—this is impossible. Rather, one can focus on God by thinking about such things as this statement of "absolute Truth":

> There is no power but God; I am the child of God, filled and surrounded by the perfect peace of God; God is love; God is guiding me now; God is with me.

This can be thought several times a day. However, one should then drop all thought on the matter until the next prayer time.

According to Fox, the golden key will, if given a fair trial, never fail to work.

## Peale's formula

Norman Vincent Peale, who wrote extensively on positive thinking, prayer, and imagery, recommended a prayer formula that is less passive and more action-oriented. The formula involves three steps:

*Prayerize.* Talk to God in a personal manner, not only about problems, but about everything in life. Pray without ceasing. Ask for fresh insight.

*Picturize.* In prayer for a specific outcome, picture your goal as happening. Print it on your mind. Believe in it. Then surrender the picture to God's will.

*Actualize.* Act as though the outcome has already happened.

In *The Power of Positive Thinking* (1952), Peale tells the story of actor Walter Huston, who visited a health club and saw this sign above the operator's desk: A P R P B W P R A A. The letters stood for "Affirmative Prayers Release Powers By Which Positive Results are Accomplished."

## *Directed versus nondirected prayer*

The jury remains out on which method of prayer, directed or nondirected, is more effective. As we saw in Chapter 4, the research of Spindrift, Inc., demonstrated that nondirected prayer, that is, for the "general good," was more effective than directed prayer, that is, for a specific result. While Spindrift's findings are impressive, they are by no means the final word. Larry Dossey, M.D., author and researcher on prayer and on alternative healing, notes, "It is not easy to employ a nondirected prayer strategy. When our health fails, we usually waste no time in telling the universe what to do."[14]

For every testimonial and experiment vouching for nondirected prayer, there are equally compelling testimonies and experiments vouching for directed prayer. People claim they have healed themselves of cancer by making very specific prayers, accompanied by vivid imageries. Others say they have done the same by handing the matter over to God to decide.

The use of one type of prayer over the other depends on the prayer and the situation. Some people feel more comfortable taking a more assertive approach to prayer, while others are more passive.

Many people who are deep into prayer life find that they gravitate toward nondirected prayer, that is, a surrender to the will of God, to the acceptance that whatever happens is for the good of all. However, there are still times when directed prayer feels more appropriate. Again, let your intuition guide you.

# A daily habit

We all pray during times of worship and crisis. Prayer, however, should extend beyond those times—it should be a part of daily life. In fact, it should be a way of life. Set aside a few minutes for prayer every morning, before the day's activities begin, and every evening, before going to bed.

Even if your needs mean your prayers are petitions and intercessions, make part of your prayer time thanksgiving. Think or speak aloud all the things for which you are thankful. Nothing should be taken for granted: health, food on the table, clothing, jobs, love, and more.

A useful exercise to help focus on thanksgiving is to draw up a list prior to evening prayer time. List ten or so good things that happened to you or that affected you during the day. Nothing is too small or trivial to be included. In fact, sometimes it is the small acts in life that make the biggest difference to us at the end of the day. No matter how grave the troubles, giving thanks for the good things helps to keep the soul in balance. It realigns our thinking to the affirming aspects of life. It mitigates despair, replacing it with joy. It harmonizes us with the flow of the universal life energy, which in turn can bring us the positive results of prayer that we seek.

It is also helpful to have a regular spot in which to pray: a room or a favorite chair. Minister Jim Rosemergy has a favorite green chair for prayer. When he is in the chair, he is automatically "turned Godward," he says.

Sometimes travel, space limitations, or unpredictable household routines make having a private "prayer space" difficult or impossible. Setting aside a space is merely a means to attune the consciousness and set a mood. There are other ways to accomplish that. One is to hold a favored object, such as a cross, rosary, crystal, stone, or anything that fosters a connection to the divine. These can easily be taken with you wherever you go.

Researcher William Parker advocated "ten steps toward a richer, fuller life." Two of the steps are to pray every morning and every night. The other eight are:

* Pray for the world.
* Pray for others.
* Pray for your enemies.
* Ask yourself daily what you *truly* desire.
* Every day spend some time alone to be honest with yourself and with God.
* Every day try at least once to be consciously with people or a person.
* Every day at least once do something to improve your environment, wherever you are.
* Every day say a definite "no" to some activity and a definite "yes" to another activity. This simplifies life, which in turn facilitates prayer.

## Life prayer

We should consider our whole life to be a prayer. "Everything you do is a prayer," agrees Silent Unity codirector Mary-Alice Jafolla. "St. Paul's admonition to pray without ceasing means always having an awareness of the presence of God in the back of your mind. We should strive for a constant awareness that we are part of something grand and trustworthy—something that we can rely on and which always works in our behalf."[15]

Make certain that your thoughts, words, and deeds are in sync with your prayers. As Charles Fillmore, the cofounder of Unity said, "In order to realize Truth and to demonstrate it, you must live it."

"We have no need to beg God for anything," says Richard Jafolla.

"We already have access to all of the good that God has for us." Affirmative prayer gives thanks for these blessings, and acknowledges that God's good is already ours, he says.

Unity teaches affirmative prayer. Our life is a prayer because God—who is Spirit rather than person, place, or thing—acts through us rather than upon us. We connect with God through our minds, yet there is ultimately only one Mind. Meditation and concentration are techniques used in prayer, which is always pitched in a positive tone. One prays by entering "the Silence," in which one seeks a direct experience of God by focusing on God, or on words of Truth, such as "God Is, I Am," or "Peace, be still." (The Silence and mysticism are discussed in Chapter 13).

Unity also teaches that we have an inheritance from God in the form of divine ideas. These are living forces that manifest through us in the world. They are: faith, strength, wisdom, love, imagination, power, understanding, will, order, zeal, renunciation, and life. Charles Fillmore, cofounder of Unity, saw these ideas as being symbolized by the twelve disciples of Jesus.

## Group prayer

In the Bible, Matthew 18:20 implies that the combined prayer of two or more persons is more effective than the prayer of a single person. Anecdotal experience seems to bear this out in many cases. Group prayer seems to create more power. Perhaps one reason is that a synergy takes place in group dynamics, making the whole of the group effort larger than the sum of its parts.

"Group prayer is more potent than individual prayer for a number of reasons," says Benor. "First, the more people there are who are focusing in the same direction for the same purpose, the more the power of the prayer is enhanced. Group prayer also invokes a group awareness, in which each person can potentiate and validate the others' belief, and thus strengthen the meditative focus."[16]

In the late 1960s Karlis Osis, then director of research for the American Society for Psychical Research, conducted an informal study of religious practices and psi with small groups of meditators. Participants often were in telepathic communication with each other and also shared the same visions. In addition, they shared a buoyancy of mood, feelings of openness and meaningfulness, and intense love.

Psychic and faith healers understand both the power of prayer and group synergy in healing. A supportive group atmosphere helps the healing process, while a skeptical or disbelieving group synergy means certain failure.

In recognition of this apparent, enhanced power of group prayer, most churches and many spiritual and metaphysical organizations have group prayer services, often called prayer circles or prayer chains. One of the largest prayer services in the world is run by the Unity School of Christianity near Kansas City, Missouri (Chapter 11).

## Factors that influence prayer outcome

The question of correct prayer versus incorrect prayer was examined in an interesting study by researcher Grant Henning, the results of which were published in 1981 in the *Journal of Psychology and Theology*. At the time of the research, Henning was associate professor at the American University in Cairo.

Henning wondered if there were underlying patterns of human behavior that could be demonstrated empirically to be associated with positive outcomes of prayer. Such patterns of behavior were likely to conform with biblical doctrines regarding how to pray, he said. The results of his study provide some interesting material to ponder. Though they were obtained from a small sample, they can, indeed, apply to a broader audience.

The subjects of Henning's study were ten American and European adults (five men and five women), who were between the ages of twenty-five and thirty-nine and who were Protestant missionaries in the Middle East. The participants were asked to self-report approximately five of their own prayers that they felt were answered and five prayers that were not. A total of ninety-nine prayers were reported. The participants rated the efficacy of their prayers according to a scale of variables devised by Henning.

The variables, all but one of which have a biblical basis, were:

*Single versus group prayer.* As mentioned earlier, group prayer is advocated in Matthew 18:20.

*Vowing.* This is a conditional prayer, in which the pray-er vows to render a service to God in exchange for his granting the petition. For example, in I Samuel 1:11, Hannah prays to God to enable her to bear a son, whom she promises to dedicate to God in return.

*Claiming a promise.* The pray-er reminds God of a previous promise to grant a petition. Numerous examples are given in the Bible. For example, in I Peter 1:4, Peter cites God's promise of an imperishable inheritance of salvation through the resurrection of Jesus Christ.

*Fasting.* In Matthew 6:18 Christ said that reward could be obtained through fasting. Thus, some pray-ers believe that fasting prior to making a petitionary or intercessory prayer will positively affect the outcome.

*Thanksgiving.* The pray-er thanks God in advance of the prayer being granted. Various examples are provided in the Bible, including St. Paul's instruction to make requests to God along with thanksgiving (Philippians 4:6).

*Agonizing.* Jesus sweated blood while he prayed in the Garden of Gethsemane (Luke 22:44). Pray-ers can experience an intense agony indicative of a struggle of will.

*Authority versus meekness.* Prayers can either be demanded of

God or sought in humility. In the Garden of Gethsemane, Jesus ultimately surrendered his will to God's ("not my will but thine be done").

*Repetition.* "If at first you don't succeed, try, try again" is the motto here. Luke 18:1–7 advocates perseverance in prayer, even when the prayer is repeatedly denied.

*Private versus public object of prayer.* Private prayer is for one's self and friends and relatives, while public objects of prayer are others beyond one's immediate life. The Bible advocates intercessory prayer in I Timothy 2:1–3, in which Paul instructs Timothy that "supplications, prayers, intercessions, and thanksgivings be made for all men" and all kings and others in high places.

*Perceived will of God.* This is a pray-er's confidence that the prayer is in keeping with the will of God. I John 5:14–15 states that "if we ask anything according to his will he hears us. And if we know that he hears us in whatever we ask, we know that we have obtained the requests made of him."

*Urgency.* This is one's level of need and desperation. James 5:16 urges people to "confess your sins to one another, and pray for one another, that you may be healed."

*Acting upon the outcome.* The pray-er begins behaving as though the prayer has been answered, before results are evident. Mark 11:24 states, "Therefore I tell you, whatever you have asked for in prayer, believe that you have received and it will be yours."

*Seeking cleansing.* This involves prayers of confession with requests for forgiveness, as well as for other results. According to Psalm 66:18, if iniquity is in the heart, the Lord will not listen to prayers.

*Outcome.* Henning's final variable was the pray-er's assessment as to whether or not the prayer was granted.

In tabulating the results, Henning found that pray-ers rarely used vowing and fasting. This is probably true of the adult Christian praying population in general. On the opposite end, the most frequent prayer behaviors were perceiving the request to be in accordance to the will of God (surrender); urgency (we usually pray the most when the chips are down); and claiming a scriptural promise (most of us are good at trying to collect what we think is owed to us).

Of the thirteen variables, Henning concluded that a weighted combination of the following ones stood the best chance of yielding desired results in prayer: acting on the outcome; thanksgiving in advance; prayer for a personal rather than public object; sensing the will of God; vowing; and claiming a biblical promise.

Some of the variables speak for themselves as obvious measures to take in prayer. Let's take a closer look at them.

*Acting on the outcome.* By believing and behaving as if our prayer is already answered, we facilitate the manifestation of our request. The Bible tells us this, and it is also evidenced by the metaphysical Law of Attraction and the power of thought, which we saw in Chapter 5 on prayer and thought. The more we engage all of our senses—by seeing, tasting, smelling, hearing, and feeling the outcome—the more power we create toward our goal. Faith and trust are the most likely factors to influence the outcome of prayer.

*Giving thanks in advance.* This is part of acting on the outcome and helps to set forces in motion toward the realization of our goal. We assume our prayer has been answered affirmatively, and we give thanks for it.

*Prayer for a personal rather than public object.* In Henning's study, "personal" meant someone who was close to the pray-er. This finding is at odds with other dominant views on prayer and healing. In group prayer, people pray for others whom they do not know personally; it is the cumulative power of the group that is believed to help the individual, rather than a personal connection between pray-ers. The success of Silent Unity (Chapter 11) certainly attests to this.

Many spiritual healers make effective healing prayers for persons they do not know and who may be far away from them. Sometimes just a first name is all that is necessary to establish a sufficient "personal" connection for the prayer. For example, Caroline M. Myss, M.A., an American intuitive and researcher, is able to make highly accurate medical diagnoses using only the person's name and address to "tune in." At Silent Unity, the pray-er needs only a person's first name in order to make a spiritual connection and to be assured that the universal mind is acting upon that request.

As Rupert Sheldrake observes in his morphogenetic fields hypothesis (Chapter 2), a connection can be established between two persons with either a name or information about a situation. Thus, we can pray effectively for strangers who are thousands of miles away in a war zone, simply by knowing about their plight.

*Sensing the will of God.* Pray-ers who try to put themselves in attunement with divine will, rather than impose their own will, are more likely to get their prayers answered affirmatively. Various testimonies to that are given through this book. This is an important factor in successful praying.

*Vowing.* Few of Henning's participants used vowing in their prayers, but when they did, they felt it brought positive results. Henning observed that women were more likely to do this than men. I believe that prayers need not be conditional; they stand on their own merits.

*Claiming a biblical promise.* The presence of this factor in Henning's results may have more to do with the fact that the participants were all missionaries and thus more likely to cite the Bible in everything that they did, prayer or otherwise.

As we can see, there are numerous factors involved in the art of praying. Not all of them are in agreement. Nor are any of them hard and fast rules. In the final analysis, prayer is a subjective experience, and each situation is unique. Perhaps the best approach can be condensed to a few simple guidelines: keep prayer simple, pure, and honest; believe that your prayer is answered; and be willing to surrender to divine will.

# *Eight*

# WHEN IT'S TIME TO SURRENDER

There are times when we realize that, no matter how or what we pray, we are uncertain of the outcome. In fact, the matter rests entirely in the hands of God. Sometimes we reach that point only after we've prayed and prayed for a specific outcome, and it hasn't happened. We finally say, "Okay, God, it's up to you. I accept whatever is your will." Other times, we pray that way from the outset, asking God to do whatever is best.

That is the prayer of surrender. But surrender does not mean giving up. Quite the contrary. Surrender is an all-win position.

## Letting go of the outcome

All of the major spiritual traditions teach the importance of detachment: we need to overcome our attachments to things and desires in the material plane before we can truly access Spirit. And when we pray, especially for certain goals and objectives, we must detach ourselves from the outcome, placing the matter in the hands of God. "Let go and let God" is one of the key tenets of many a philosophical platform, including that of Alcoholics Anonymous. "This or something better" is often spoken at the end of prayers by many persons in acknowledgment that what God has in mind may not be what the prayer desires. As many of the persons in these pages attest, we are fooling ourselves if we think we know what is absolutely the best course of events for ourselves and others. The big picture, constructed by the Master Architect, is not visible to us; we see only tiny portions of it. Therefore, when we pray, it is certainly all right to have certain objectives in mind, but ultimately we must leave the outcome up to the divine order.

"If we begin with the assumption that God wills for us to be whole and that in fact his desire for our healing is even greater than our own, then our approach to prayer is not so much a matter of striving as it is of yielding," says Lawrence W. Althouse, a minister, healer, and former national president of the Spiritual Frontiers Fellowship International. "Instead of trying to get across to God what we want him to do for us, we will concentrate more on putting ourselves in his hands so that he may do with us as he wills."[1]

Althouse relates the story of a woman who wanted to avoid an operation:

Sometimes people will assume that if they have faith in God, they need not see a physician. I was asked to visit a parishioner's friend in the hospital. She was suffering from a dangerous kidney disease, and her physicians were talking about a kidney transplant, which frightened her terribly. "Pastor, please pray for me so that I won't have to go through a transplant," she said desperately. "Isn't it true that if I have enough faith, I won't need it?" "Not necessarily," was my reply. "Mary," I continued, "did you ever stop to think that God uses many different means to accomplish his purpose? I truly believe he wants you well, but I'm not about to tell him how he must accomplish his own purpose."

Mary looked very doubtful, but I continued, "It may well be that God intends to heal you through the kidney transplant. That also takes faith, you know." Mary sank back against her pillow and was silent for what seemed a very long time. Finally, she looked at me and said quietly, "OK, I'll try. Would you pray for me as you think best?"

As I prayed I had the feeling that if Mary could let go and permit God to use whatever means he wanted to use, she might not need the kidney transplant. Her willingness to commit herself to God's love might be the key to her healing. I said nothing of this to her, and when I left the room I was unsure of what direction her faith was taking.

Several days later she called me on the telephone. Her voice was ecstatic: "I don't have to have the operation, and the doctor says I can go home tomorrow!" I cannot know what were the dynamics that produced that happy result, but I am convinced that Mary experienced healing because she came to realize that God heals in many different ways and through many different people.[2]

## Letting go of illness

In healing, prayer cannot be effective as long as someone has a need to hold on to an illness or problem. On a deep level of consciousness, some people do not wish to be healed. Perhaps they get attention as a result of their illness, or perhaps they can duck certain responsibilities. Ann Marie Davis, who battled Hodgkin's lymphoma from the age of ten (Chapter 1), believes that she unconsciously sought cancer as a way to opt out of life at an early age. She is now fully healed of that inner wound.

"All healings involve an element of the person being healed having a willingness to let the pain or problem go, and having a belief in the power of the healing to help," says Daniel J. Benor, M.D. "Once I was working with several other people in the Reiki tradition. We did a laying on of hands with a woman who had severe arthritis of the thumb. She'd had this for two years and had had injections and other treatments, and nothing would relieve the pain more than temporarily. In one healing, the pain went away. She came off the treatment table purring because she hadn't been able to touch her thumb and other fingers together in two years. She said, 'Where's my pain?' That was the wrong thing to say, because in a few hours she brought the pain back. She realized that she was holding on to that habit, and she had to release the pain. It took several more healings before it left permanently."[3]

Kai Kermani, M.D., a general practitioner and spiritual healer in England (Chapter 6), tells of what he calls "a classic example" of a woman with advanced cancer:

> She'd had cancer for four years. She'd been doing very well and suddenly her cancer had gone completely crackers. She'd been to all sorts of different therapists, and then she came to me.
>
> During her fourth healing session, we got talking and it came to me intuitively that I should ask her, "Why can't you let your cancer go?" She came straight back, "He's been my good buddy!" Then she said, almost in shock, "Did you hear what I said?" I said, "Yes." So, she'd been considering her cancer as a friend against which she couldn't fight! And she'd been totally unaware of that. She said, "I'm not quite sure if I can get rid of him. He's been a good friend to me; he's changed my life."
>
> Now that she's facing the crunch, she doesn't know whether she wants to work on herself or not. It requires taking responsibility for yourself.[4]

## Skepticism and denial

The literature on healing abounds with stories of skeptics who experience miraculous healing. One famous example was told by the renowned American faith healer Kathryn Kuhlman in her biography by Allen Spraggett, *Kathryn Kuhlman: The Woman Who Believes in Miracles* (1970). Kuhlman had lectured audiences on conditions that had to be met in order to be healed: faith, belief in God, and so on. "Then one day I got the shock of my life," she said. "A man said his deaf ear had just been opened in a service, but he had no faith at all. 'I don't believe it,' he said, 'I never go to church.' Well, there went my theology out the window."[5]

Nonetheless, skepticism and denial are powerful inhibitors to the healing power of prayer. "Disbeliefs can probably block healing from occurring," agrees Daniel J. Benor, M.D.

Consequently, if we truly wish to benefit from the healing power of prayer, we should discard skepticism—or at least be open to the possibility of being healed.

Minister Lawrence W. Althouse tells the story of a skeptical woman whom he was called to heal. The woman, whom he refers to by the pseudonym of "Mrs. Thomas," first came to see him for counseling following the death of her son from illness. Despite her desire for help, Mrs. Thomas was doubtful about faith in God and the power of prayer. The counseling thus wasn't able to advance, and after a while, Althouse and Mrs. Thomas mutually agreed to stop the sessions. Some months later, Althouse received a call from a friend of Mrs. Thomas's, who told him that she was in the hospital due to have surgery to remove a growth on her neck. The friend asked him if he would visit her. He agreed, albeit somewhat reluctantly, remembering that the counseling had been ineffective. He recalls:

> Greeting her as I entered the hospital room, I said, "Your friend suggested you might want me to pray for you." "Sure," Mrs. Thomas replied good-naturedly (her skepticism was never hostile), "why not? It can't do any harm." With that encouragement, I placed my hands on the growth, prayed briefly, and beat a hasty retreat. I had done what I was asked to

do, but I didn't expect anything would happen. Mrs. Thomas was too doubtful, I was sure.

The next day her friend called me and informed me that the operation had been postponed. It seemed that when the doctor visited Mrs. Thomas later that same day when I had called on her, he found that the growth on her neck had shrunk some, and he decided to postpone surgery until it was determined what would happen. I was incredulous at this news but even more so a day or two later when the same friend informed me that Mrs. Thomas had been discharged from the hospital. The reason: the growth had disappeared! Of all people I thought might be likely recipients, Mrs. Thomas, the pleasant skeptic, seemed one of the most unlikely. Apparently, God knew something I didn't![6]

Though skeptical, Mrs. Thomas at least had opened herself to the possibility of healing through prayer with her agreement, "Sure, why not? It can't do any harm." Would her tumor have shrunk if she had hung on hard to skepticism? It is impossible to know.

We should not let unnecessary obstacles come between us and the healing power that can come through prayer. Rather, we should open our hearts as much as possible to divine love and trust in the unfoldment of divine will.

## "I didn't get an answer until I let go"

Chris Jackson grew up in the Unity church and was taught from an early age that prayer is a real and tangible power. He was ordained a Unity minister in 1989 and now is executive vice president of the Unity School of Christianity. He is a tall man of striking appearance, with thick dark hair, clear brown eyes, and a resonant voice that serves him well in both speech and song.

Over the years, Chris has put prayer to many a test. His experiences have taught him much about himself, about God, about prayer, and about the true order of highest good that exists in the universe. During one of the lowest points in his personal life, prayer enabled him to rise to a higher level of consciousness that expanded his spiritual worldview and brought about a healing in his relationship with his wife.

I visited with Chris in his office, which was pleasantly filled with plants and personal mementos of experiences and trips. He explained his prayer philosophy and talked about his recent healing experience with prayer.

"Our understanding of prayer is constantly developing," Chris said. "Prayer meets the need at whatever level the need is expressed. I really believe that. That's what makes every prayer powerful. Fortunately, the universe does not depend on us understanding how prayer works in order for it to work.

"What I have found in my own personal experience is that as soon as I think I know what prayer is, it becomes like a chameleon and it changes on me. My concepts of prayer shift as my concepts of God, or my consciousness of God, expands within me. Throughout my life, I have had major shifts in the way I understand prayer and in the way I pray—the way I activate prayer consciousness within myself.

"For most of my life, prayer was a way to obtain things. Sometimes they were noble things—health or feeling good or something for another person. It was meaningful and valuable for me at that time in my life. But as I moved along, that kind of prayer became unfulfilling. It was time to move into another understanding.

"My most recent understanding of prayer is that there is really only one prayer: 'Purify me, heal me, and use me.' Over the past few years, I have come to believe that we don't know what is good for us, let alone what is good for another person. Yet we pray as though we do know what's best—that's the prayer of supplication. All I can say is, thank God that many of my own prayers didn't come true, because they weren't ultimately for the highest good.

"I want to make it clear that I don't discount prayers of supplication. There are still moments in my life when I will use that kind of prayer. When you're in the dark night of the soul or in great desperation, you need what you need, no doubt about it. I would never tell a person who called Silent Unity asking for a healing, 'Are you sure it's in the highest good?' I would pray with that person, because I know the prayer will be understood within the larger scheme of things.

"Personally, I find myself moving more and more into the prayer of awareness. That is, to open myself as completely as possible through prayer to being purified, healed, and made an instrument for God. That awareness came out of a personal experience when I went through a family crisis that lasted over two years.

"It had to do with my wife and I separating, and the havoc that comes out of that. I didn't want the separation, so I sought desperately to pray and pray and pray that we would come back together. I pleaded with God for that specific outcome. It didn't come to pass. I didn't get an answer to my prayer until I finally let go. The answer was totally different than the one I wanted . . . and I felt let down, if not betrayed, in a sense, by God.

"But then another piece of my awakening in that experience was to realize that betrayal, which we think of as negative, is really self-betrayal, of an old way of thinking, an old consciousness. Those old ways will always betray us. We're not here in life to stagnate, we're here to progress. So my feeling of betrayal by God actually led me to a new understanding of God. Betrayal was a gift.

"I could see then how my prayers really were a form of manipulation. They were coming out of an old consciousness, in which I wanted to control—I wanted things to be a certain way. I wasn't really trusting that there was a higher, grander plan at work. I was almost forced to make that shift. Once that happened, I was lifted to a whole other understanding of prayer.

"Ultimately, my wife and I did reunite. I had been ordained as a

Unity minister in 1989. At the time of our separation, she had entered the Unity ministerial program. It was a time for her to expand her consciousness. Evidently, we also needed time to spend on our own spiritual paths before we could come back together.

"The real good, the real *God*-ness, of that experience never went away. It was there all the time. It was just my perception that couldn't grasp it, but that was exactly what had to happen. Until I could let that happen, there was no chance of us ever coming back together again. I'm convinced of that. Based on my old consciousness, the kind of partnership we have today couldn't have happened. It had to do with a broader, more spiritual understanding of what it means to be in a relationship with another person.

"I love Unity and Unity teachings with all my heart. But we come out of a school of mental science, which says that if you speak an affirmation, if you hold a thought in your mind, it will produce after its kind. That's true. But we must be careful that we are not really just playing manipulation games with the universe. We're seeing a lot of that in the world—a material manipulation that's based on the desire of 'let me use all of these tools to get whatever I need.' The law of mind action *will* work that way. But there is a much higher way in which we can pray.

"I grew up in Unity, and I was told that if you think the right thoughts, you will have the right life. This became part of my theological crisis. When my family was falling apart, I had to think what I had done to bring this on. I realized that a lot of mental science students get caught up at that point. They begin to blame other people or blame themselves. I was blaming myself, thinking I had not been a good Christian, or a good Unity student. Since then, I realized that what happens to us in life is not nearly as important as how we respond to it."

I asked Chris how prayer takes us through gateways in consciousness so that we can reach the higher levels he spoke about.

"The first key is humility," Chris answered. "Then willingness and surrender. In any of its forms, prayer always forces us to recognize a power greater than ourselves. Prayer lifts us to a place where we can see that there is something greater working in the universe. When a person has that realization with a humble and willing heart, it can lead us right through from one level to another.

"It can be blocked by nonwillingness, nonreceptivity, or a person who is not in a space of humility. Fortunately, the universe does a splendid job, and spirit will bring us to our knees in order to learn our lesson. That's what happened to me in 1992. For a long time I was not willing to humble myself and let go of my ideas and concepts of who I was. So I had to be brought to my knees in order to see that I was something much greater than who I thought I was.

"Humility is often a hard lesson! It is difficult to do, and the mind is a master at fooling us into thinking we have reached a point of detachment."

"Where does prayer fit into the big picture, the grand cosmic scheme of things?" I inquired.

"I think humanity as a whole is progressing to a higher consciousness," said Chris, echoing a widely held view. "We will either do it willingly and joyfully, or we will be pushed into it. That's the evolution of the universe. I believe we are on the threshhold of an evolutionary leap. There is less predictability and dependability in the world, and so people are being pushed, sometimes with great force, to break out of that old way of thinking. Human consciousness has been at the prayer supplication level, but it is beginning to move higher. Certain people are having experiences that are waking them up to a new way of living. They are the pioneers who need to move the whole human race. I believe this has been happening for quite some time. [Unity founders] Charles and Myrtle Fillmore were pioneers, in that their ideas on prayer were at the time very bold. If they were here today, they would want the rest of us to continue in the same bold ways. We're getting ready to make an exciting shift."

Chris's story hits home for a lot of us. Who hasn't had ups and downs, or crises, with a spouse or partner, or perhaps faced the prospect of losing an important relationship? How difficult it would be to surrender to a course of action contrary to what we would anxiously want. But as he points out, often we can't see the greater wisdom of an answered prayer until it plays out.

## The question of free will

It may seem that surrendering to divine will means surrendering one's free will. Does divine will imply a preplanned path or cosmic decisions made out of one's reach?

The answer is no. If we are truly in attunement with God, then free will and divine will are one and the same. It is only when we are out of attunement that divine will seems imposed upon us, and we struggle against it.

Prayer is one of the most direct ways for us to reach this attunement. When we reach it, we know it, through the subtle hummings of the soul.

Is it possible to be constantly in attunement? Mystics and adepts the world over, throughout history, have spent lifetimes striving to do so. However, we can improve our attunement in daily life by making prayers of surrender and by being willing to accept the outcomes of those prayers.

# Nine

## "Pure Unconditional Love"

It took end-stage kidney failure for Maurice Williams to appreciate firsthand not only the tremendous power of prayer in healing but the tremendous healing power of unconditional love. When his kidney failure was diagnosed, Maurice was given hours to live. Survive he did, but then he had to face years of ups and downs with health crises. His victory inspired him to conceive the "Five Steps to Systematic Healing," which he teaches in workshops he gives all over the world.

A big man with a booming, friendly voice, Maurice hails from Chicago. After moving to Detroit in the 1970s, he discovered Unity and enrolled in its ministerial program there in 1979. Here is his story:

"I was a carpenter, I was robust. I had just enrolled in the Unity Urban Ministerial School in Detroit. I was working ten to twelve hours a day and going to ministerial school. In 1981 my energy suddenly started running down. I didn't have an appetite. When I went to the doctor, he sent me to the hospital immediately. They told me I had kidney failure and that I needed to have an operation immediately and go on dialysis. I couldn't believe it! I was in denial. I wanted to think about it awhile, pray on it. They said, 'You have less than twelve hours to live. You need to make a decision *now*. One of the best surgeons in the Midwest is available today. We want you to have him.' "

Maurice had no choice. If he wanted to live, he had to undergo an operation and begin dialysis. The surgery, which took four hours, involved attaching a vein and artery together in one arm. That created Maurice's literal lifeline, the place where the machine would be connected to draw out the accumulated poisons in his blood.

Dialysis can be an exhausting procedure. Three times a week, the patient must be connected to the machine for four to five hours. Severe fatigue usually follows the treatment, even into the next day. Just as the patient begins to feel good again, it's time to go back for another dialysis, and the cycle starts over. Life becomes dependent upon the machine. Travel cannot be undertaken without consideration of where the nearest dialysis facilities are, and if they will be available.

"I did not like dialysis," Maurice acknowledged. "When I was on the machine, I never once looked at the needle in my arm—I refused to identify with it. I listened to gospel tapes and read instead."

Maurice was able to continue in the Urban Ministerial School and then joined the Unity Ministerial Education Program at Unity School for Religious Studies at Unity Village, which is near Kansas City, Missouri. Then in 1983 the good news came that a kidney was available for transplant from a cadaver—a man who had been killed in an auto accident. Maurice went into the hospital with high hopes that the transplant would be successful. Back at Unity, his classes were praying for him, as were many others. James Dillet Freeman, Unity's resident poet and former director of the prayer ministry, called Maurice and prayed.

But Divine Will had other ideas involving other people in Maurice's life. To Maurice's tremendous disappointment, the kidney failed.

"That tested my faith," he said. "The doctors told me, 'Well, we tried.' My classmates asked, 'What happened? We prayed.' In the back of my mind, I knew that the kidney had to work, because prayer works. God heals.

"Weeks later, I was still on the dialysis machine, and I was getting despondent. I asked a nephrologist why they didn't take the kidney out since it wasn't working. Then I said it *had* to work. The doctor said, 'Of course it's going to work. You don't need another kidney.'

"That was all I needed to hear. It was like the angels were telling me at my lowest point to have faith. A week or two after that, one day while I was on the machine again, I was told the kidney had started working, and it was sufficient enough to take me off dialysis.

"That kidney lasted about four years. I was ordained a Unity minister and went to Nassau in the Bahamas to open my first church, which grew to more than one hundred persons.

"Then I started to feel bad again, losing all my energy. I flew back to Kansas City and doctors told me that my body was rejecting the kidney and it could not be saved. I had to go back to Nassau to announce that I needed to give up the church in a month, because fluid was building up in my body and there was no technology in Nassau to help me deal with the situation.

"When I arrived at Nassau, that was where my power of faith really came in. While I was waiting for my bags at the airport, one of the church members who'd come to pick me up said, 'Maurice, why don't you heal yourself?' I had never thought about that. She said, 'You're a healer, so heal yourself.'

"I thought about how we do have the power to heal ourselves, because Jesus said, 'according to your faith, not mine.' That was my turning point.

"Healing yourself doesn't mean you're going to go without a kidney.

It means changing your mind. Stop looking at the problem and start looking at the solution, which is wholeness. So that's what I started doing. Instead of leaving Nassau in a month, I stayed until the end of December. I found a nephrologist there. Even though the kidney was failing and the fluid was building up in my body, I was able to keep on working, giving seminars, doing weddings and christenings, right up to December thirty-first.

"As soon as I returned to Kansas City and checked in at the hospital, they put me on dialysis immediately and removed about twenty pounds of fluid. I took a sabbatical from the ministry. I was hurting, having had to leave my first and favorite church.

"It was then that I had a battle with God. I always encourage people to go with their emotions and not be in denial. You have to process your emotions to be whole and healthy. Don't linger in them, but go through them. We want faith to win in the end, and it will. I had to work through a lot of emotions about why this was happening to me."

It was at that point that other members of Maurice's family were drawn into the situation.

"Meanwhile, my sister from Chicago came forth to offer me one of her kidneys for transplant. The doctors tested her, and everything seemed well, until we got to the chest X ray, and she was shown to have a little mass on her lungs. It prevented them from taking the kidney, because you have to be in excellent condition. She didn't know she was not breathing to her full capacity, but only about sixty-five percent. Even though I could not use her kidney, she was able to straighten out her problem. The mass was not cancerous. If she hadn't been willing to donate a kidney, who knows how long it would have been before this other problem would have been noticed. Maybe it would have gotten a lot worse. It goes to show you that when you're willing to do something great, something great happens in return.

"Actually, my brother Eric, in Detroit, had the perfect kidney. But he was obese, and he had a weird lifestyle. He did everything that was fun. I had always thought I was healthier than he was, because Eric was a good-time man. My mother kept telling me to call him and ask for his kidney, but I wasn't about to do it. Finally, though, I did. I had nowhere else to turn. He surprised me by saying, 'Sure, I'd be glad to do it. I was waiting for you to ask.'

"I still worried that he would be healthy enough, but the doctors approved him. You see, your prayers are always answered, not necessarily the way you want them answered, but the way that it is best for you.

"Eric arrived for the transplant on July twenty-sixth, 1987. He got off the plane in this three-piece suit with buttons missing in the center. That meant he was still overweight. I was worried again. Now, Eric never goes to church, knows nothing about the Bible, but he's a spiritual man. He looked at me and said, 'I came here to give you a kidney, and I'm not going to leave until I do. I'm here because I love you.'

"We went into surgery on July twenty-seventh or twenty-eighth. Eric went in first. To remove the kidney, they had to go in through his back and cut across to the front and take out a rib. It was a tremendous surgery, more complicated than mine. Before we went in, we looked at each other, and he said, 'I'm giving you this kidney because I love you, and God is giving you this kidney because he loves you.' It just wiped me out.

"The doctors said that as soon as they put the kidney in my body, it started working immediately. The next morning, Eric was walking down the halls, flirting with all the nurses. He was out in six days, a record time. I was out in seven. Normally, it would take weeks for major surgery like that. He was supposed to take off work for two months. He was only off a month.

"The whole thing was amazing. Eric gave me that kidney and he set me free. No conditions. No calls to me to remind me, no asking for anything. Just pure unconditional love. I keep him in my prayers daily. Last July it's been seven years, and I'm still in great health."

After the second transplant, Maurice took a position as senior minister with Unity Southeast in Kansas City, Missouri, and then joined the staff at Unity School for Religious Studies at Unity Village as an instructor. His experiences with prayer and healing have been an inspiration to his coworkers and students and to the audiences he addresses around the world.

"I learned some tremendous lessons," he said. "I had to let go of what I wanted to happen. All I had to do was accept God's will, and let it go naturally, and the process took care of itself.

"One thing that happens when you have challenges is that you develop more compassion. You move right into a different world. Life takes on a different value system. I think about how cocky I was before then, so confident about everything, including my body—I wouldn't eat right, I hardly ever exercised. I abused my body in a lot of ways, which I don't do now.

"My prayer life has changed drastically. Once you reach your extremity, when you get to the point where nothing else seems to work, then you really start working with prayer. Not only did I work with prayer, it became a habit. My prayer became one of gratitude. Prior to my kidney failure, I always prayed for something. Now I pray to give thanks. Prayer is giving thanks for what you already have. You don't get what you want, you get what you already have. Time is something that we impose. Praying for something to happen in the future only delays it; for example, I am already healed, all I have to do is catch up with it. Jesus said that whatever you pray for, if you believe you have received it, you will.

"Every day is a day of grace and enjoyment for me. I don't take anything for granted anymore, I take everything in stride. Everything is a blessing. Even those times when things are not going my way, a prayer of gratitude turns things around and makes them go much better."

Maurice's "Five Steps to Systematic Healing" are remarkably simple, yet most effective. They can be applied to any crisis, be it health, relationship, financial, whatever. The five steps are:

1. Forgiveness: No *permanent* healing without forgiveness.
2. Faith: You must believe.
3. Action: Faith without movement is stagnation.
4. Thanksgiving: Give thanks *before* demonstration.
5. Proceed: You can't go forward looking back.

Forgiveness is so important, Maurice stresses. "It opens our closed eyes and enables us to see what God is offering us," said Maurice. "We must learn forgiveness in order to heal."

Maurice's realization that what we pray for already exists echoes the teachings of mystic Joel S. Goldsmith. Said Goldsmith: "Here is the great secret of prayer, that God is All-in-all and God is forever manifested. There is no unmanifested good or God. That which we seem to be seeking is ever-present within us and already manifested, and we need to know this truth. All good already is, and is forever manifested. *The recognition of this truth is in answered prayer.*"[1]

## Love, prayer, and health

Spiritual healers describe themselves as channels for the universal life force or for God's energy. These are different terms for essentially the same thing: love. Healers are channelers of love. Many of them are also described by others as loving people—they are first filled with love in order to bring the healing power of love to others.

The Polish-born healer Mietek Wirkus, who now practices in Bethesda, Maryland, sees healing as the movement of energy through the heart chakra. "Heart center vibrations relate to unconditional love, and to treating other beings with love, understanding, and respect," he says. He adds that the healer "must feel and be the heart chakra. . . . It is not thinking the word 'love,' it is not a visualization process, it is the real sensation of pure love which brings warmth, delicate vibrations in your heart area."[2]

Love promotes and restores health. We've known that for millennia—witness the testimony of healers, mystics, philosophers, and artists. Love has universally been described as a powerful, redeeming, healing energy.

In recent years, with the rise in alternative healing modalities, we have come to appreciate the role of love in health and healing in general, not just within the confines of spiritual healing. "If I told patients to raise their blood levels of immunoglobulins or killer T-cells, no one would know how," says Dr. Bernie Siegel in his book, *Love, Miracles, and Medicine* (1986). "But if I can teach them to love themselves and others fully, the same change happens automatically. The truth is: Love heals."[3]

One way love heals is through prayer. Prayer itself is based on love: self-love, love for others, love for community, love for the highest good, love for God, unconditional love. Through prayer, we can all become transmitters of the universal life force, or love.

# Ten

# PRAYER, DREAMS, AND VISIONS

The answers to prayers do not always come to us as thoughts, the whisperings of the inner voice, or intervening events. No, the answers do not always come in the physical plane at all. Instead, we find ourselves transported to otherworldly realms. We may behold exquisitely beautiful scenery, beings of light, and formless, dazzling white light. Or, we may find ourselves in strange and exotic territory, where "reality" is askew. If we were ill or near death before we left on these journeys, we might return to find ourselves miraculously healed. We have had a vision or had a dream, and it has made us whole again.

Why are some prayers, especially for healing, answered in this way? The answer is one of God's secrets—it is the mysterious working of the universe. Perhaps it has to do with the expansion of human consciousness toward a higher level. God, or the Universal Mind, reveals itself through increasingly spiritual and intimate experience. The remote Absolute becomes more personal when expressed as spiritual beings such as angels and guides or experienced as a beautiful place such as heaven.

The literature on the near-death experience (NDE) documents cases in which NDErs return from their heavenly journey healed of major illnesses and life-threatening traumas. During their trips, they encountered angels, spirits of the dead, religious figures such as Jesus or the Virgin Mary, and even God. In a classic NDE, they arrive at a beautiful place, usually after traveling through a tunnel toward a brilliant white light, and are met by a figure or figures who convey to them that they must go back to their bodies and earthly life. Usually, no specific reason is given, other than that there is unfinished business.

Author David Engle recounts the story of a woman named Janet who became seriously ill with polio in 1952. By the time she got to the hospital, she could barely walk, swallow, or breathe. Her limbs became paralyzed, and she lost consciousness. In her NDE she went to a spiritual plane, saw her dead grandmother, and was attracted to a heavenly light. She then realized she had to return because it was "too soon" to die. With great effort, she returned to her diseased body—and immediately awoke able to breathe and swallow. She recovered.[1]

In another example, a woman named Catherine lay in a hospital in 1970 dying of Hodgkin's lymphoma. In her NDE she went through a tunnel, at the end of which was a figure she knew was God. She begged him to let her stay, but he gently pushed her away, telling her there was something she had to do for him before she could come to him. She was so upset to find herself back in her body that she willed herself back into God's presence. He held her and said, "Do you understand?" She indicated she did, and this time returned to her body and regained consciousness. She was completely cured of cancer.[2]

Not only are people healed in such visionary experiences, but they also emerge from them healers themselves. Kenneth Ring, Ph.D., one of the foremost researchers of the NDE, states in *The Omega Project* (1992) that, according to studies, NDErs are two to four times more likely than others to have healing ability, psychic gifts, electromagnetic sensitivities, and other characteristics. The NDE, says Ring in another book, *Heading Toward Omega* (1984), is "a brief but powerful thrust into a higher state of consciousness," the effects of which "resemble those that stem from a mystical experience." (This subject will be discussed more in Chapter 14.)

Divine healing also comes in dreams. Sometimes information to bring about a healing is given in dreams by angelic figures who appear as doctors or nurses or as wise old women or men. Sometimes the healings themselves seem to take place in dreams. "Your dreams can help keep you healthy, warn you when you are at risk, diagnose incipient physical problems, support you during physical crises, forecast your recuperation, suggest treatment, heal your body, and signal your return to wellness,"[3] says Patricia Garfield, Ph.D., psychologist and a leading authority on dreams. Garfield says that when we are ill, our dreams change—they become loaded with a symbolic language reflecting our state of health.

Ancient wisdom holds that we actually travel to a dream state—a real place where dream events play out. Sleep opens the door to an alternate reality, quite often a surreal version of our waking reality. All rules of time, space, and logic are suspended in dreams. In dreams we transcend the boundaries of our waking consciousness to experience consciousness on more subtle and subjective levels.

The early Greeks and Romans believed that when the body was asleep, the soul became free to travel to a "between state" wherein dwelled the lesser spirits who mediated between humans and the gods. Here the human soul could have experiences and encounters that had the same validity as experiences had during waking life. What made the dream experiences more special, however, were their supernatural characteristics. In dreams it was possible to meet the gods, to see the future, and to be healed of illness and disease.

The healing power of dreams was especially revered in ancient times. The Greeks established healing temples devoted to the god Asclepius, where the ill came for ritual dream incubations. Since dreams were regarded as real events and not imaginary, the conditions were created at these temples to induce dreams that would cure the individual's complaint. If a dream included certain symbols associated with Asclepius, such as an olive tree, a serpent, a bearded man, or a handsome youth (especially associated with miraculous cures or a rejuvenation), then the dreamer would be cured. Sometimes the god Asclepius himself appeared in a dream to heal the patient. If the person did not have a healing dream, then he or she sought to receive the cure through a vision.

When you pray for healing, do not forget to examine your dreams for answers.

## An angel guides the radiologist

Besides appearing in dreams, angelic figures literally project through humans, such as medical professionals. Garfield cites an example of a woman who believed her spirit guide channeled through her doctor on one occasion when she needed reassurance. Similarly, I was told the following story:

John from Rochester, New York, is an emeritus associate professor of English and an ordained Spiritualist minister. He received his bachelor of arts degree from Princeton and his master of philosophy degree in the philosophy of religion from the Joint Program in Religion of Columbia University and Union Theological Institute. He is a trustee of the Academy of Religion and Psychical Research and has contributed many articles and reviews to its journal.

John's first experience in the psychic-spiritual realm occurred at age seventeen with precognitive clairvoyance. Five years later, he experienced trance channeling and ecstasy. These experiences shaped the rest of his life. John began studying with an esoteric teacher.

Today, John and his wife, Grace, a United Church of Christ interim minister, are well known for their lecturing, preaching, and work with groups in esoteric philosophy, meditation, and spiritual healing. John is at work on a book about his own perspective on noetic experience. (Noetics is the study of consciousness.) Their daughter, Rose Christian, is a clairvoyant and uses her ability in her work as a physician.

On December 28, 1993, John found himself frightened on an operating table. His prayers for help brought angelic intervention.

The previous August, John had suffered a transient ischemic accident (TIA), or minor stroke without detectable consequences, while attending a writer's conference at Cape Cod. It was a Friday night, and the conferees had just finished dinner. Sitting at the table, John felt the whole room tilt. Actually, he wilted, falling toward the floor. His son, who was sitting next to him, caught him, laid him gently on the floor, and then helped him to a car. They sped to a hospital, where John spent three days recuperating. Doctors told him he could go home and recommended that he undergo ultrasound tests to determine the condition of his carotid arteries, which are the main carriers of the blood to the brain.

John had the ultrasound done. Results showed that one carotid artery had a blockage of between eighty and ninety-nine percent. John could have surgery to enlarge the artery. But first, his internist wanted to do an angiogram to make certain that there was no deterioration of the arteries of the brain. If there was, there would be no point in doing the surgery. Apparently, the internist was relying on earlier studies that pointed to a high risk factor in carotid artery surgery; the risk now is considered to be very low.

The internist sent John to doctor after doctor after doctor for test after test. Meanwhile, John's anxiety level rose, and he suffered two more TIAs. Finally, the angiogram was scheduled to be done in a hospital in late December 1993.

To produce an angiogram, dye is introduced into the arteries, which then reveals the condition of the arteries on X rays. To get the dye to the arteries of the brain, it is carried up by a probe, which the radiologist inserts in the iliac artery in the groin. When the probe gets as high as it can safely go, the dye is released, and the X-ray camera goes to work. The patient is conscious throughout the entire procedure, in order to respond to the radiologist's requests to shift the head and neck positions. Angiograms must be done carefully, for a mistake can result in another stroke, possibly a fatal one.

From the outset, things did not seem right from John's perspective. The young radiologist began by reciting the customary official warnings of the dangers to life in this procedure. He did not seem to be in a pleasant mood, and his voice was cold and uncaring. John felt his body begin to shiver. He later learned that his blood pressure, normally around 125 over 80, escalated to over 200. The radiologist continued to talk while he prepared himself. He related stories about his personal life. He upset John by complaining that the operating room was too cold.

After more than an hour, the doctor successfully completed the angiogram on the right side of John's body. John sighed in relief. He thought the procedure was finished, because the preliminary report had indicated that it was the right carotid artery that was problematic. He told the doctor, "Good, congratulations. It's over, and I have survived. Thank you."

The radiologist replied, "Not so fast, I have to do your left side too." John was dismayed, but resigned himself. The radiologist began on his left arterial path. Soon he stopped. He showed noticeable concern, John thought, and indicated he wanted to consult a colleague about the next move of the probe. The doctor called the nurse and told her to immediately fetch a radiologist who was working in the adjacent operating room.

John was genuinely frightened and began to pray in his mind for help. *Please help this man solve the problem,* he prayed over and over.

The other radiologist arrived, and John kept praying. He heard his radiologist tell the other one what the trouble was. His voice stopped for a moment, and then John heard him speak again, this time in a voice filled with relief and confidence. "I've got it," the radiologist said. "It's okay."

A half an hour later, John's radiologist had completed his examination of the brain arteries on the left side. The angiogram was at last over. He slowly withdrew the probe and then for some minutes held his hand at the point of incision to stop the bleeding. While he did so, he removed his surgical mask, and John was astonished to see a marvelous sight. The face he saw was not the rather ordinary human-male face of his doctor, but a new face, transformed and radiant. It was the face of an angel, right out of a medieval painting. It was neither male nor female, but simply angelic. The beauty was so astonishing, so incredible, that John could not believe his eyes.

John believed that his prayer had indeed been answered. But how could the face transposed over that of his doctor's be explained? John thought that it had to be either the inner, spiritual face of the doctor himself or else a being that entered the doctor at a crucial moment to safely guide the angiogram. This being could be a spirit or departed human—or, it could be an angel.

These thoughts shot through John's mind as he gazed into the angelic countenance and offered a mental prayer of thanks, which he directed with all the intensity he could muster to this sacred person, this saving being, spirit or angel—but probably angel.

The entire procedure took nearly three hours. John was put to bed in the recovery room. About an hour later, his radiologist entered to see how he was doing. As John looked at him, he felt a surge of friendship for him. His face, however, was no longer that of an angel, but his familiar mortal one. It seemed clear to John that this radiologist had been taken over by "someone else" for the duration of the procedure, and this "other being" had helped guide him.

A week later, John had a successful operation on his carotid artery.

The angiogram experience was so incredibly marvelous that, following the surgery, John wrote to the radiologist to tell him he had something remarkable to share about their joint experience in the operation room. The radiologist did not answer the letter.

Perhaps it is just as well; the mystery should remain a mystery.

John still marvels at the radiant face he saw gazing down at him and how his whole being was flooded with gratitude. "Was I thankful," he said. "Was I *thankful!*"

## God spoke to her

The following is the story of a bedridden woman who heard the voice of God and was healed. It was published as a broadsheet around 1769, entitled, "An account of the remarkable recovery of Mrs. Mary Read, of Rehoboth, to the use of her limbs, of which she had been deprived three years":

Mary Read having been confined to her bed three years successively, namely, from June 1766 to June 1769, and never walked a step; on the 24th day of July 1769, as she lay meditating, these words came to her like a voice audibly spoken, "Daughter be of good cheer, thy sins are forgiven thee, arise and walk." They were repeated three times over, which caused her to think it was the voice of God speaking to her by his Word and Spirit. But this question was put in her mind, "How do you know it is the voice of God?" With this suggestion, it is not the voice of God. Then she doubted whether it was God's voice or not; upon which these words came to her, "It is I, the Lord that speaketh unto thee, fear not." She, still hesitating about the matter, said, I trust that God spoke to me by Way of Command." The words were repeated the second time, "It is I, the Lord of Hosts, that speaketh unto thee, arise and walk, fear not." As she was greatly solicitous to know whether it was the voice of God or not, the words were repeated over the third time, "It is the Lord of Hosts, the God of Israel that commandeth thee, arise and walk, fear not." This was backed with the words of Samuel, "Behold, to obey is better than sacrifice, and to hearken than the fat of rams." This confirmed her that it was the voice of God, and his almighty power. For while the words were repeating, the use of her limbs were restored to her again; the cords and sinews on one side of her, which had been shrunk up six or seven inches, for so long a time, were then stretched out, and she became straight, and received strength, and immediately rose up from her bed and walked! And now she desires that all people would praise God for this miraculous and glorious deliverance vouchsafed unto her. Afterward the 55th Hymn of Doctor Watts's, in the first Book, was brought sweetly to her mind.

It's almost amusing that God had to boom at Mary Read three times before she paid attention. The story bears a striking similarity to a modern-day one that follows, in which an angel instructs an impaired woman to get up out of bed and walk.

## The angel said, "Get up!"

Joan's life fell out from under her the day her house burned, and she narrowly escaped with her two daughters. The fire was the beginning of a downward spiral: surgery to remove a cyst, followed by a diagnosis of cancer, and then complications from more surgery that left her partially paralyzed in one leg. Despondent, unable to walk, and in chronic severe pain, Joan felt her will to live gradually seep out of her. And then one night her prayers were answered—by an angel.

Before the fire in 1982, Joan lived the average American middle-class life. She lived with her husband and two girls in a comfortable home in the rolling countryside. The house had been built by her husband, Don,* and herself. Joan did volunteer work at school, held a part-time job at a day-care center, and was busy with all the domestic demands that raising a family bring. Physically active, she loved to work in her yard and garden.

"I just ran with life and believed in God," Joan, a pretty brunette in her forties, told me one evening as we sat in her living room. "I took the girls and went to church regularly. I felt good when I was at church and I loved to be there. I prayed all the time—you know, for protection and for the girls, things like that."

The fire occurred on March 10, 1982. "We had a wood stove in the basement," Joan said. "That night the smoke alarm went off. I thought it was a chimney fire. I was counting money for Girl Scout cookies, or I would have been in bed at the time. Don wasn't home. I went downstairs, looked around, but couldn't see anything. The alarm went off again, and I went to the basement, where I found the ceiling burning. The damper had stuck, and it just got so hot it melted the electric wires in the basement and everything caught on fire. Everything was black. Flames began coming through the register next to one daughter's bed. The electricity went out. I got both my daughters out—they were in third grade and kindergarten at the time. I ran next door and got help. Then I went back to get the animals out, but I could not touch the metal door to get it open. It was too hot. But I had my girls out.

"The house did not burn to the ground. The fire chief asked me why, because most houses would have burned completely. I told him my husband and I had built it. He said, 'You must have built it airtight. Another ten minutes and it would have blown up to get air.'

"What really upset me the next day was seeing the smokeprints of my daughters' bodies in the beds where they were sleeping. Then I knew how close we came to not making it out. I felt like it was my fault because I didn't figure it out soon enough. But I realized the most important thing—that my girls were safe."

The fire destroyed Joan's sense of safety and security. Suddenly life seemed very fragile. "It changed my outlook on life," she said. "It's like I held on to fear—I didn't feel safe anymore. And I didn't care what happened to me. I quit going to church. I quit believing in God. I just put a wall up and quit.''

Joan also quit praying. "What protection, whatever had kept me at peace, just wasn't there anymore,'' she said. "I didn't have the ability to bounce back from anything anymore. Everything seemed big and upsetting.''

Joan and Don rebuilt their house. It was a strain, with work and everything else that had to be done to run a family. During the same time, Joan's stepfather was diagnosed with lung cancer, which added to family stress. Joan soon began to feel that she could not cope.

In August of the same year, Joan had surgery on a pilonidal cyst near her tailbone. Many people are born with pilonidal cysts and never are troubled by them. Joan's cyst began bothering her, and so she had sought medical help. At this time a biopsy revealed it to be benign.

Just after the surgery, the couple moved to a new home in the same area.

"Things seemed to be normal for a while,'' Joan recounted. "I worked with my husband a lot. Then I started to lose my energy and I wasn't interested in doing anything at all. I thought something was wrong with my mind. I felt like I had the flu all the time. Just vacuuming the house made me want to crawl into bed. I didn't look forward to anything. Even my children seemed to bother me, and normally I enjoyed them.''

One night, Don noticed a little lump at the top of Joan's left leg. Within a mere two weeks, it had grown noticeably in size. Joan returned to doctors, who ordered a biopsy. But Joan already intuitively knew the verdict: the lump was cancerous. The biopsy confirmed that.

After that, a nightmare of consultations and tests began. Joan was sent to a dozen different doctors at five hospitals. The doctors believed that the cancer was originating from the pilondial cyst previously diagnosed as benign. Radiation and chemotherapy were rejected in favor

✳◉◗◉◗◉✳
PRAYER,
DREAMS,
AND
VISIONS
—
141

of exploratory surgery which at the least would remove the tumor and the nearby lymph nodes at the top of the leg.

The diagnosis of cancer was frightening to Joan. She kept thinking about her stepfather and how she'd visited him in the hospital every other day as he lay dying, watching him waste away. She vowed to herself, "Okay, I'll fight and make it through this." She began to pray again. "I prayed not to leave my kids until they were old enough to take care of themselves," Joan said. "I prayed, 'Please, God, let me stay until they can manage on their own.' I also prayed to live at least long enough to see them graduate from school."

Prior to the operation, an ominous premonition surfaced in Joan's thoughts. "The day before the surgery, I was really upset," she said. "I went for a walk. The doctors had told me that one of the risks of taking out the lymph nodes was that my leg might swell up big, and the swelling would not go away. I knew in my heart that something with the leg would go wrong, and it wouldn't be swelling. Walking down the road, I didn't think that I would be walking like that again. I didn't know exactly why I felt that way.

"When I came to after the surgery, I was in terrific pain. It felt like someone had put a vice right across my toes and wound it shut. At one point, I think I was screaming that my leg hurt, because my voice seemed to echo inside my head."

Something indeed was wrong: a blood clot had formed in the leg, and Joan was rushed back into surgery to have it removed. "They got the blood clot out, and when I came to, the pain was not as bad. I thought, 'Gee, that's a little better here. I don't I feel like I need to scream.' "

But something else was wrong: nerve damage. "I noticed that the toes on my left leg weren't sticking up," Joan said. "I looked at my foot, and my toes were under my foot! I was purple up to my knee. Then I started feeling the pain again. They put me in intensive care and kept me on a heart monitor for a couple of days. They were afraid I'd have another blood clot.

"My mother had a fit. She asked for a board to straighten my toes out. They weren't going to do anything—they were going to leave my toes just dangle. I wanted to try to get my toes back up. I couldn't work my foot at all. I couldn't even wash it, because I could not stand water on my foot. I couldn't stand the bedcovers on my foot."

Joan was given therapy to learn how to walk with a walker. She had to wear nylon support leggings whenever she got out of bed. The leggings were so tight, she said, that "it took two nurses and me to get them on. I had blisters on my knuckles from trying to pull these things on. On top of it, I was nauseated a lot from the pain. I had a hard time keeping food down. I usually bit on my covers, and then I'd chew on ice, and I wouldn't get sick. That's how much it hurt. My foot felt like there was a heartbeat in every toe. It tingled like pins and needles or like a bee sting."

Joan was in the hospital for fifteen days. She learned how to clean her wound herself and how to pump out the fluid that would build up in her leg. She was home only a couple of days before she had to return to the hospital to have an absess in the wound taken care of.

At home, Joan was in agony from the nerve damage to her leg. She had to keep her bad foot propped up because of its constant throbbing with pain, despite the pain medication she was taking. A trip in the car to see the doctors was a major ordeal. So much as placing her foot on the floor of the car while it was in motion sent her reeling with pain. She hobbled around with the aid of a walker.

The doctors told her there was nothing they could do to reverse the nerve damage. But Joan was determined to regain her ability to walk. "Pushing with the board, my mother and I worked on my toes every day so that they would stay up where they belonged," she said. "They didn't go under the foot all the time. You can't walk if your toes keep falling under your foot. But I was pretty depressed. I thought, 'Okay,

I've made it through the surgery and all the things that had went wrong, but I can't walk, and I'm stuck in my room. What am I going to do now?' "

The situation seemed hopeless. In mounting despair, Joan became increasing despondent. The pain made her irritable and difficult to get along with, straining her relationship with her family. Due to her inactivity, she gained weight, quickly adding on forty pounds. She couldn't sleep at night. She felt miserable. "I got to the point I couldn't stand my own kids around me," Joan said. "They were ashamed of me. They wouldn't push me in the wheelchair or help me. They were mad at me for being sick. I had a real guilt trip, because I knew I wasn't very pleasant to them. I didn't even like to hear their voices, and that really scared me! I thought, 'You're in bad shape if you don't even want to hear your own child.'

"My mother couldn't have been better, but she would take me places and answer questions about my condition to others. I was embarrassed. I finally realized I had to get a grip on this. Who wants to live like this?"

A cousin from Delaware who was trained in Reiki asked Joan if he could give her healing. Joan agreed, although she knew little about energy-transfer healing. But at this point, she was willing to try almost anything for relief. She would sit outside in a recliner chair, and cousin Carroll would give her Reiki. The sessions always relaxed her and made her fall asleep. With every session, Joan began to improve.

Then one day Carroll introduced Joan to a woman, Judy, who worked with crystals in healing. "She brought a whole bunch of stones," Joan said. "She said to me, 'We're going to try to do a healing with you.' I thought, 'Yeah, sure! With stones!' I wanted to laugh."

The session amazed Joan. Judy placed crystals on her body and told her to relax. During the course of the healing, Joan found herself talking about all sorts of emotions she'd repressed, some for most of her life. There was hurt over her early family life: she was alienated from her father, and her parents separated by the time she was in third grade. There were blocked feelings over a speech impediment Joan had suffered as a child. There was sadness and guilt over the death of a younger sister at age fourteen, a sister she had promised never to leave. There was resentment and anger over the conflict between some members of her family. That and more came roiling to the surface, to Joan's amazement.

"I heard my voice, I heard me talking, but my eyes wouldn't come open," Joan said. "I rattled on. I was getting all this junk out that I carried around. I must have poured everything out, except for some blanks in my childhood that I don't remember, I guess because of my daddy. I don't know. I think that's how I've protected myself. If I went into my own little world, none of it could hurt me. So I blacked things out myself.

"I must have said everything in the world that I ever thought about or heard. Afterward, Judy burned some incense that she said was for purification. I thought a lot about all the stuff that had come out. I felt a bit guilty over some of it, but I thought, 'Well, I've got to let that go. But what's next? I still can't get out of my room!'"

Nonetheless, Joan worked diligently on letting go of past hurts. She listened over and over again to a tape for cancer patients by Louise Hay, author of *You Can Heal Your Life*. The tape helped her in her emotional release.

Joan didn't realize it then, but she had hit bottom. She was in pain, imprisoned by a wheelchair and a walker, overweight and unhappy, and filled with repressed negative emotions. The Reiki and crystal work helped clear away the rubbish, and her prayers and determination gave her the fortitude to keep trying. The stage was set for the road to recovery.

"Finally, the letting go of all those feelings stopped one day," Joan said. "My mother came, and then she went out for a while. I went to sleep. I prayed to God. I said, 'I'd rather die than keep on living like this.' I think I only slept a little while. Suddenly I heard this voice. A beautiful voice, a man's voice. It kept saying, 'Get up!' And then again, 'Get up!' I thought, 'What do I want to get up for?' But the voice kept pushing me, so I finally sat up on the side of the bed. 'Get up!' the voice said. I thought, 'Okay, I'll just do this so you'll leave me alone!'

"I stood right up next to the bed! I thought, 'What am I doing!' I hopped around, looking for my walker. It wasn't anywhere. Then a light appeared in the room. It was like the sun shone! I kept looking out the window for the sun, but instead the house kept getting lighter and lighter and lighter and lighter. There was no corner, nothing that didn't have light coming from it!

"I *walked* down the hall. By myself, without a walker or anything. I thought I must be dreaming, but immediately I knew I wasn't dreaming, because I could still feel the pain and tingling in my foot. I said to myself, 'I can't be dreaming! I am walking!' I came out to the living room and stood by the bannister to the stairs. I wanted to run outside. I wanted to run out and say, 'This is beautiful! I love it! This is beautiful!' We didn't have many neighbors, but I thought if anyone saw me, they'd have me hauled away.

"I stood by the bannister for a while, and then I realized that I had the ability to go down the steps. I walked up and down the steps three times! I thought, 'This is terrific!'

"The light was still filling up the house. It was so bright, but it didn't hurt my eyes. I felt weightless.

"Then I thought, 'No one will ever believe this. Wait until Mom comes back.' I went back to my room and sat down on the bed. I thought, 'Well, who do I call? What do I do?' But something just kept telling me, 'Keep it to yourself, keep it to yourself. Just think about it. Keep it to yourself.'

"I thought that if this was a dream, I would be well. I would never be sick again; I can walk. Then the voice said—and this is where I get a lump right here in my throat still—it said, *'I am with you.'*

"I lay back down on the bed and went right back to sleep, as though I'd never been up. It was a real peaceful sleep. I don't know how long I slept. When I woke up, I was in a bit of a relaxed daze.

"When Mom came back, I tried to get back up. I couldn't stand. I thought, 'This is a real joke to do to somebody!' Then I was really depressed. I didn't tell Mom or anybody what had happened to me."

Joan thought about her experience for a long time. The only conclusion she could reach was that she had been visited by an angel. The experience instilled in her the knowledge that she could walk again—somehow, if she just kept trying.

"I found that I was more peaceful in general," Joan said. "I'd go see the doctors, and they'd tell me that I was going to be a lady of leisure now, because I wouldn't ever be able to walk normally again. I'd say to myself, 'Not me!' I let it all go. No matter what these doctors said to me, I knew it would be different. I didn't pay much attention to them. The kids commented how good it was that I was nice again. I didn't realize how mean and nasty I'd been."

Joan was fitted with a brace for her bad leg but still was not given much hope for recovery. Meanwhile, a friend, Hazel, who is a massage therapist and trained in Reiki healing, began to work with Joan. Hazel lived closer to Joan than her cousin Carroll and soon weekly treatment sessions showed a vast improvement to Joan's leg. The treatments included massage, Reiki healing, chakra energy work, creative visualization, and talking out problems in her life that had kept her from moving forward. "That was the real turnaround for me. The more we worked, the more we got the leg to work. The foot would ache like crazy for a couple of days after Hazel worked on it. But we knew we were making progress. She worked with me a long time, and finally I was able to walk again.

"I would walk as much as I could in the house with the brace on, no matter how much it hurt. I did that for months. Then I was able to get in a car and drive myself. That was a big deal! I could go to the grocery store by myself. I was still dragging my foot, but I was walking on my own."

The visitation by the angel also opened up psychic abilities in Joan. She took classes in extrasensory perception. There she met people whose metaphysical studies and experiences validated her visitation by the angel.

Though the angel with the masculine voice did not return, other angels arrived, offering guidance and intuitive promptings to keep her on the right path, she said. Joan now senses their presence often. "I have actually seen them. They have no faces. I see light in shapes that most people would think angels look like. There are always two, one behind the other. One guides me in what I say. I didn't talk much when I was growing up. Now I've learned to talk and know that I have the right to say my opinion, as long as I do it kindly. The guide has almost become like my body. When I'm talking and thinking things out in my brain, I can feel it right there next to me, helping me. It's gotten that close with me.

"It's a female presence. I got the name 'Lacy.' The color yellow comes with her. *L* is for love; *A* is for Alicia, my older daughter, who has been through a lot; *C* is for caring for others; *Y* is for you—you can bring change into your life."

Joan proved to be a quick study in the classes in psychic development. She learned how to clairvoyantly see and clear auras. She began to meditate and take classes in Reiki healing. She also returned to work fulltime, in a day-care center in a church.

Joan also felt reconnected to God and resumed going to church—a healing church rather than her former Lutheran church. "Church is very important to me again," she said. I go to a healing ministry, and I love it. We meditate and I can see the most beautiful purple and gold colors. No matter what has gone on that week, it makes me feel that I can sweep it all out, start over again. It just feels so good! I know the angels and God hear me. I've learned one of the basic lessons—you don't get help from Him unless you *ask!* And I've learned to ask!

"You can pray anywhere. You can pray mowing the lawn, sitting in the car. You can pray eating your lunch. It doesn't have to be a special place. God is with you all the time. You also need to give thanks every day, no matter how bad things look.

"One of my dreams was to talk to somebody about this whole experience, and tell them everything," Joan said. "I knew it was coming."

✗●✗●✗●✗
PRAYER,
DREAMS,
AND
VISIONS
—
149

# Eleven

# THE NEVER-ENDING PRAYERS

One of the major prayer centers of the world rests right in the heart of the United States. There is no grand shrine, no wall, no grotto, no cube to mark the spot. Nor are there throngs of pilgrims to be seen sending their prayers heavenward. Yet millions of people from around the planet—from all religions and from all walks of life, from the mighty to the meek—seek out this prayer center every year. Some seek it out of desperation, in a last-ditch attempt to save a sinking ship in life when all other measures have failed. Some seek it out of faith, fully confident of the miraculous power of prayer.

The prayer center is Silent Unity, one of the cornerstone ministries of the Unity School of Christianity. It is part of the campus of Unity Village, which lies just on the outskirts of Kansas City, Missouri. The prayer center staff works around the clock, twenty-four hours a day, three hundred and sixty-five days a year, praying with anyone who calls or writes for assistance. No request is too small.

The requests pour in by the millions every year. Each one is handled with personal attention and held in strict confidence. There are no catches, no strings. No counseling or advice, no confessional judgments, no solicitations for donations, no requests to send representatives to your home to save your soul. Just prayer. Offered by a compassionate man or woman who gives no personal name, but speaks only in the name of Silent Unity.

What do people want prayers for? Overwhelmingly, for health problems. Also for jobs, for strength to overcome substance abuse, for strength to leave abusive relationships, and for mending broken relationships.

One night, a teenaged girl called from a public phone booth on a Los Angeles freeway. She had run away from home and had gotten involved in drugs and prostitution. She wanted to go back home, but when she called her parents, they told her to stay away. Her next call was to Silent Unity. "What do I do now?" she asked in desperation.

The pray-er could not advise her, but he could pray with her that she would be guided to do the right thing. Although she clearly wanted someone to tell her what to do, she was calmed by the prayers.

Before the next sunrise, Silent Unity received a call from a halfway house on behalf of the girl. She had gone to them that very night for help, and they in turn had taken her to a substance abuse treatment center. She had one request: "Please call Silent Unity for me and let them know that our prayers have been answered."

People call for prayers when they are down on their luck. A woman caller said she had no money and her farm was going to be auctioned off the next day. After the prayers she said, "I have faith that God is going to move." Move God did—the area was hit by one of the worst snowstorms ever the following day, making it impossible for the sheriff to come out and hold the auction. Somehow, during the day's grace, the woman got enough money to stave off foreclosure. She called again to say thanks. (Silent Unity points out that prayers are made for the resolution of problems in whatever way God chooses to work, and are never for such things as divine manipulation of weather.)

Another woman called just as she and her four children were on the brink of eviction from their apartment. Later, the landlord called her, apologized for his anger, and said she did not have to move.

Another woman told a pray-er, "You don't know what it's like to be all alone and to know that you can pick up the phone and there will be a caring voice on the other end. You must all be angels."

People also call to pray for those who suffer from famine, war, and oppression in troubled places around the world. They pray for the resolution of political crises and for souls who cross over in great tragedies and disasters, such as plane crashes and hurricanes.

They pray for sick and lost pets, and pets who must be put to sleep. One woman calls every now and then for her canary, who likes to sit on her shoulder and sing while she prays. Another woman has a German shepherd who howls in the background whenever she calls Silent Unity.

Children pray for sick parents—the youngest anyone recalls was a girl of four who called on behalf of her "sick mommy." Sadly, many children pray for their parents to stop drinking or for beatings and sexual abuse from parents and relatives to stop. People hovering on the brink of suicide pray to hold on to life.

The prayer works, regardless of whether or not people are desperate, or skeptical about the power of prayer. Perhaps it is no accident that Unity rests within the Show-Me state of Missouri. The testimonials, received daily at Silent Unity via phone and the mail, speak for themselves. They're called "good reports," and some are published (anonymously and with permission) in *Daily Word,* Silent Unity's monthly inspirational magazine.

The good reports cover every conceivable situation. Most deal with serious health matters such as cancer, heart problems, detached retinas and major operations. A common good report concerns prayers for impending operations to remove tumors. People testify that after the prayers, the tumors miraculously disappear and the operations are canceled. Another common type of good report are those concerning successful risky surgeries and faster-than-normal recovery rates. Other good reports cite success in finding jobs, in overcoming alcohol and drug abuse, in healing relationships, and in surviving disasters.

The escapes from disasters are particularly intriguing. People call Silent Unity in the midst of a natural disaster to pray to be spared. One woman reported that a tornado bearing down on her house did an about-face after she called Silent Unity. A family threatened by a raging fire in California sent a photograph testifying to the power of their prayer: nothing inside their white picket fence was touched by flames, yet everything around them burned to the ground. A woman in a hurricane in Florida testified that her house was spared, but houses around her were blown to pieces.

People also call Silent Unity in the midst of their own personal crises. A woman called while suffering a heart attack. She said she was going to call her doctor, but she wanted to call Silent Unity first. She reported feeling an immediate sense of peace. Another woman called in the midst of a miscarriage. The bleeding stopped while she prayed with a pray-er on the phone.

## Myrtle's brainchild

As we saw in Chapter 5, the Unity movement is the result of the spiritual awakenings of Charles and Myrtle Fillmore through prayer. The Fillmores hosted a small group of dedicated persons who came to their home every evening to pray at ten P.M. In 1890, a year after Unity began, Myrtle announced the creation of a new department called the

Society of Silent Help. It was an expansion of their at-home group. People everywhere were invited to join the prayer communion at ten P.M. their local time. The purpose of the prayer sessions was to meditate upon the living reality of God until it became a living reality in their minds and hearts.

Every month, a prayer affirmation was published in the Unity magazine for all pray-ers to focus upon at the appointed hour. The first one was:

> God is goodness and everywhere present. He is the loving Father, and I am His child and have all His attributes of life, love, truth, and intelligence. In Him is all health, strength, wisdom, and harmony, and as His child all these became mine by a recognition of the truth that *God is all.*[1]

The Fillmores believed strongly in the power of united prayer. The Society of Silent Help was an immediate success. Letters began to pour in from people who were sick, unhappy, or seeking spiritual fulfillment. The bigger the society grew, the more the Fillmores realized just how powerful united prayer could be. It had unlimited potential. In 1891, when the Fillmores changed the name of their magazine to *Unity,* the Society of Silent Help became the Society of Silent Unity and has been known since as Silent Unity. The appointed hour was changed to eleven P.M. to accommodate more persons.

In addition to wanting to join in the prayer circle, people wrote letters to ask for specific prayers to help them. Initially, almost all of them dealt with healing matters. Then financial matters began to show up, and as the movement grew, people felt freer to request help for all kinds of situations and problems.

The published prayer affirmations in the magazine took on an almost mystical power. At first called "Class Thoughts," they were expanded to two a month, one to cover healing and one to cover prosperity. For a few years in the early 1900s, they were printed on a tear-out sheet so that readers could take them out and carry them around. The sheet was red and became known as "the red leaf." People would rub the red leaf on parts of their bodies that were in need of healing—and reported successful results.

Prayer affirmations are still published in *Daily Word*. They are no longer called "Class Thoughts," and there are now four each month, to cover inner peace, guidance, healing, and prosperity.

As the telephone became more commonplace, an increasing number of persons called in their prayer requests. The Fillmores often fielded many of the calls themselves, then added staff to do so. Prior to World War I, the telephone service became around-the-clock. Eventually toll-free lines were added.

Today Silent Unity receives 1.9 million letters and more than 1 million telephone calls (not all are for prayers). Those numbers are growing every year.

A staff of one hundred six persons works in the telephone prayer room. They come from all walks of life and all types of professional backgrounds. They are specially trained for this job. Those who work on the telephone lines have books of prayer affirmations to fit virtually any situation; they turn to these as each call comes in. The prayers, says Richard Jafolla, co-director of Silent Unity, "have weathered the test of many years." Incoming calls are taken by the first available staffer. They do not give out their names, and callers cannot request a particular staffer. This anonymity keeps the emphasis on prayer.

Every letter that comes in is blessed as it is handled. Everyone who includes a name and address gets an answer. To those persons who call and likewise leave a name and address, Silent Unity sends out a letter. First-timers receive a little booklet, "A Manual of Prayer." All prayer requests are prayed over for thirty days in the prayer vigil chapel.

The energy generated by Silent Unity was tangible to me even at a long distance, and I knew I had to visit Unity Village in order to experience it firsthand.

## Inside the prayer room

Unity Village, spread over a 1400-acre campus, looks like a Mediterranean villa. The buildings are stucco with red tile roofs and arched doorways. Flowers and greenery wave in the ever-present breeze. A beautiful fountain graces the garden courtyard. On top of the building that houses the chapel, there is a cupola where the lights are lit twenty-four hours a day—a spiritual lighthouse sending prayers out into the universe as beacons of love. These lights have burned for the better part of a century, since before World War I (not always at the same location), and to those who gaze up at them, they are "the light that shines for you"—literally, for everyone around the world.

My visit to Unity Village coincided with the Day of Prayer, on September 1, 1994. This was a first-ever event for Unity: to raise human consciousness by inviting people the world over to focus on prayer on this particular day. Special activities were held at Unity Village, including a twenty-four hour prayer vigil in the chapel to read aloud the names of all those persons who wished to be on the prayer list. The list included 142,000 persons who wrote in and 9,100 who called in.

Even Mother Nature joined in the event, by producing some glorious late summer weather, as well as a mysterious crop of crocuses (a winter flower) that bloomed in a garden where no crocuses had ever bloomed before.

There was another special occasion to this event. Due to the confidential nature of Silent Unity, access to it has been restricted in the past. Even some of the high and mighty in religion had only been able to peek in the windows of the telephone prayer room and the prayer vigil chapel. Now I was honored to be the first writer in a long time, and one of the few writers ever, to enter the telephone prayer room and to meet and talk to some of its staff members (because their work is confidential and done in the name of Silent Unity, I am using pseudonyms for the staffers quoted).

And how gracious they were. I was at once impressed with their warmth and sensitivity—and their energy. By their description, they have the best jobs in the world, because every day or night, every hour, every minute, they can experience the good that prayer brings others.

"Most of our work is uplifting, and the rewards are evident immediately," said David, a telephone prayer room worker. "We really don't have burnout in the prayer room, because we have opportunities to leave our stations and go off to a quiet area and recenter ourselves. We learn the secret of letting everything flow through us. We're here to pray. In fact, when we go off-duty, we're more energized than most people when they leave their jobs. Some nights we get such uplifting calls, we float out of there on cloud nine. It's God in action, it's Spirit, it's a miracle that happens right there on the phone."

David is an effervescent man who came to Silent Unity from a substance abuse counseling background. "I'm a recovered drug addict and alcoholic and have been in a recovery program for thirty-four years now," he frankly acknowledges. "I discovered Unity when I was directing a drug and alcohol counseling program in New Jersey. Someone gave me a gift subscription to the *Daily Word* magazine. As a result, I came out to Unity Village to attend some continuing education program courses in spiritual counseling and prayer for my own spiritual growth. I went back to New Jersey and found myself little by little doing more prayer work than counseling. Finally, it got to the point where almost every session would begin and end with prayer. The results were phenomenal. I took a year's sabbatical. There was a temporary position open in the telephone prayer room part-time. The next thing I knew I was on full-time.

"When I first got into the twelve-step program, it was my goal to do the will of God as I understood it. Here at the prayer room, the opportunity is so much greater for me to do that. This is such a people ministry, it has so much integrity, it's so vast, it reaches so many people. The results are so overwhelming. The greatest recommendation is that it works."

David chuckled at the recollection of his very first call as a pray-er. "My wings were all buffed and my halo was all polished, and I was filled with zeal. I said something to the effect, 'Here I am God, your faithful worker. Send me your most needy, your most troubled.' Well, he did, all right. I answered the phone, 'Good morning, Silent Unity, how may we pray with you today?' A loud, angry voice came over the line and said, 'You're a no-good-son-of-a-bitch and you're going to burn in hell!' I sat there for a moment, stunned, and then I said, 'Rest assured God loves you. And so do we.' There was a second's pause and then a timid voice said, 'Thank you.' And I said, 'Thank you, God.'"

Many first calls involve great trauma and create a kind of baptism by fire for the novice pray-er. Gayle, a telephone prayer room worker, related, "My first call was a woman who was taking her husband off of life support. She asked whether or not she should do this. She had never called Silent Unity before. I couldn't counsel her, but we prayed and prayed."

A longtime staffer, Angela, said her first call "was a ninety-three-year-old woman who cried all the way through the call. Tears were coming down my cheeks too. I was so upset that afterward, I went up to my supervisor and said, 'I don't think I can do this.' She said, 'Yes you can, dear, you've just been initiated, and you passed the test.'"

Angela went on, "Another call I'll never forget as long as I live was from a man in prison on death row. He was going to go to the electric chair. He wanted to die in peace. He knew he was guilty, and he had all these fears about the execution. He had heard about the currents of electricity and what would happen to him, and he was terrified. The family of the person he killed were going to be there to witness his death. He wanted to die in peace and he wanted forgiveness.

"I felt a lot of emotion inside, especially an overwhelming love—love that just flowed. When he said currents, I thought of a prayer we have about the 'mighty currents of God's healing love flows through you now, making you whole, well, and free.' I was strongly guided to use that prayer with him. Spirit started to flow through me as I spoke, and he started weeping. He said, 'I have to tell you, I don't know anything about your ministry, I don't know anything about God or Jesus, but all I can hear in my head is, *Today you will be with me in paradise.* Lady, I don't know who you are, but when I get to heaven, I'm going to tell Jesus about you. I know I can go in peace.' Such a feeling of love came from him. His voice changed, he felt forgiven, and he knew he could face the people.

"About two months later, another call came in that I happened to get. It was from a man in the same prison. He said he'd had a roommate who'd called Silent Unity before he was going to the chair. He also was on death row, and he couldn't forget the peace that was in his friend after the call. In fact, the local newspaper had carried an article saying 'Man goes to death chamber in peace after calling ministry in Missouri.' It was a tremendous experience."

Sooner or later, all pray-ers receive phone calls concerning dying. David told of a particularly poignant one. "A woman was in her final days of life with terminal cancer and was in a great deal of pain—the morphine wasn't doing her any good. She called her family together. She had all her affairs in order. She called Silent Unity for prayers for a peaceful passing. While we were praying with her, she looked up at her children, smiled and made her transition."

The seriousness is tempered with humor. Everything in Silent Unity is undertaken in the anonymous "we." It is so ingrained that once, a pray-er sneezed while taking a call and said, "Excuse us."

"Once I was praying with a man who was suicidal," said Angela.

"He was being very harsh and rash. I had the hiccups. I started to say, 'Sorry.' He said, 'Pardon me, ma'am, but did you just hiccup?' He laughed and said, 'You need prayers more than me!' It took the edge off the crisis. Another time, I was talking to a woman whose mother had a critical health problem. I had to sneeze, and kept trying to control it. I started to apologize, but she said, 'Don't you dare. My mother comes from the old country, where every time you sneeze, it means an answered prayer.' Sometimes," Angela said, "God has a sense of humor."

The telephone prayer room itself is modest in appearance, looking like many modern offices. It is hexagonal in shape, and decorated in soft tones of mauve and cream. The pray-ers work at small desk stations with their prayer books and writing materials. In the center of the room are huge overstuffed teddy bears that are ever-ready for hugging. Around the lighthouse-like ceiling are the names of the twelve apostles and the qualities that Charles Fillmore ascribed to them: faith, strength, wisdom, love, imagination, power, understanding, will, order, zeal, renunciation. Soft New Age or classical music sometimes is played in the background.

Though modest in appearance, the telephone prayer room is a powerhouse of energy. One can feel it, just stepping across the threshold. It is the energy generated by prayer and by the universal life force of unconditional love. It throbs, it pulses, it hums. "I can feel it especially at night," says Richard Jafolla, who makes frequent visits to the prayer room with his wife and co-director, Mary-Alice Jafolla. "The power of united prayer will knock you over. It evokes a lot of emotions. There is such a feeling of peace and love—hearing the hum of the prayers, and knowing that people are being helped, that sometimes I almost want to cry."

I visited the telephone prayer room both during the day and at night and felt a distinct difference in energy between the two. This was confirmed by staffers. An extra intensity comes over the room at night.

Perhaps part of it is due to the thinning of the veil between the worlds at night, when forces and energies "out there" can impinge more easily upon our consciousness. Perhaps part of it is due to the nature of the calls. The night shift gets the bulk of desperation calls, suicide calls, batterings, drug abuse, the down-and-out-and-on-my-last-leg calls. Night, especially the middle of the night, is when tortured souls tend to walk ragged edges, and look into the abyss.

Interestingly, these desperation calls also fluctuate according to the phases of the moon, with an increase just before, during, and after the full moon. Folklore has long held that the full moon brings on madness, though science disputes that. Nonetheless, a substantial body of anecdotal lore attests to a lunar influence upon mood and behavior.

There are many prayer services, both denominational and nondenominational, that offer prayers in much the way that Silent Unity does. Simply to be aware that people are so engaged in prayer around the clock is an inspiration to us all.

## Angela

Angela (a pseudonym I chose for her because she is so angel-like) is an open channel of love and compassion, which flow out in her anonymous voice over the telephone. The voice is the only thing callers have to relate to when they call for prayers. In her, Angela conveys far more than mere words.

Angela's ability to tune in to the needs of her callers comes from a life of hard knocks. She has weathered tremendous turbulence in life, and has come out on top, healed and whole and with a zest for growing spirituality. Prayer was and is part of her own healing; now she uses prayer to help others heal, too. In telling her story, I do not single her out as representative of the telephone prayer room staff. Her experiences are compelling, and would be compelling no matter where she worked.

Today Angela is fifty-something, a dark brunette with a ready smile and a selfless, giving manner. "Everything I've been through was preparation for the work that I am doing now," she said.

As a child, Angela grew up in a small community where she was very shy. At age eight, she was molested by family friends, which caused her to withdraw even more. It damaged her relationship with her parents, and, later, with men. She suffered from poor self-esteem and had difficulty in trusting others.

"I'd gone out with my parents to visit some friends of the family," Angela recalled. "They lived out in the country. They had two sons and a daughter. We went to play. Before I knew it they had me down on the ground. I thought they were just joking around. The girl and one boy held my hand, and they did everything except penetrate me. I was petrified. I never said a word to anybody. I must have buried it deep inside. Whenever my parents wanted to go over there to visit, I got hysterical.

"The recall of that just came out a few years ago, as a result of prayer. I knew something was happening in me because I'd have outbursts at the littlest things. I prayed and asked the Holy Spirit to help me heal, because I didn't know what it was. Then the memory started coming back."

The recall helped put in perspective Angela's difficult relationships with men. She rarely dated in school and felt lonely and unloved. In her early twenties, she met a young man who showed some serious interest in her. She was so hungry for love and affection that she responded by giving her all. A pregnancy resulted, and the young man left her.

"I went into a home for unwed mothers for about six months," Angela said. "I had a baby girl and I kept her. She was a joy. She taught me about love. But when she was about seven months old, she died unexpectedly of spinal meningitis. She'd been very healthy. I came home one day and she was very ill. I got her to the hospital, and two days later, she was gone. I was sitting in the corridor and I heard them call for a doctor. I intuitively knew what it was. I went in her room and picked up and held her and told her I'd never regretted keeping her. Then she died.

"After that, I was just numb. I kept all of the feelings inside myself. I had no one to share them with. I went on a rampage of hatred. I'd been raised a Mormon and believed that God was punishing me for not being married. Then I got involved with the Jehovah's Witnesses, who said it was the Devil, not God. Then I got involved with Unity. Really, Unity saved my life.

"To pay off the hospital bills, I worked as a beautician, and then went to work part-time in a bar. After I started, a man began coming in, and he would ask only for me. He was in his forties, tall with reddish dark hair and glasses, and had very piercing eyes. He was always in a suit, very dignified. I can still see him to this day.

"He would tip me a quarter for each drink and then leave me a twenty-dollar bill at the end of the night. One night he gave me a bill. I walked away and looked at it. It was a hundred-dollar bill. I took it back to him and said, 'I can't accept this.' He said, 'Yes you can. You don't belong here. I know you're here because you have to be. When you're done doing what you have to do, get out of here.' Because of him, I was able to get that debt paid off. After I quit, no one ever saw him again. Now I know he was an angel."

After the death of her child, Angela lived carelessly and wrecklessly. She began to have a sense that someone was watching over her, protecting her despite her carelessness.

Two abusive marriages further had damaged her self-esteem. Her first husband always managed to make her feel guilty for his temper outbursts, and she would apologize for being responsible for his behavior. The second husband she once had to fend off with tear gas. It was not until years later, when she began to pray with battered women who called Silent Unity, that she realized that accepting blame for being a victim is part of the battered syndrome.

Angela began the difficult job of regaining her self-esteem, through prayer, inner work—and joining the Toastmasters, which helped her to feel confident on her feet before an audience. She began giving workshops on empowerment for women.

"We get a lot of phone calls from battered women, including some who want to stay in the relationship no matter what," said Angela. "We never counsel, but when I'm praying with them, they tell me there is something that makes them feel that I really understand what they are going through. Sometimes they weep. I can feel a healing taking place. I'm being used by God to help these people. Even though I can't talk about my own experiences when I'm working, my essence goes out and communicates on some level with them. It's like a little saying we have: 'the wounded part in me understands the wounded part in you.' While I'm talking, I bathe them in total love and light, and tell them how wonderful they are. Sometimes I don't have to say much. People can be in such despair when they call, and in a minute or two they are uplifted. I'm here to remind people who they are. I ask God to help me bring forth what these people need."

About eight years ago in the middle of the night, Angela received a divine inspiration for working with battered women. This affirmation came to her:

> I am a Beloved Woman and I'm loved with an everlasting love. I'm worthy to receive the highest and best possible in every area of my life.
> I claim my good now.
> Thank you God for answered prayer.

Angela has herself experienced the healing power of Silent Unity prayer. In 1989 she moved to Pennsylvania for a brief period of time. There, she suffered a broken shoulder.

"I'd never had a broken bone in my life, and I was petrified at the hospital," she said. "I didn't have my own doctor, and everything in my life looked as bleak as could be. While I was waiting in the emergency room, I got up and called Silent Unity. The voice that came through was like an angel. He prayed with me, and I felt a peace come over me. I sat back down to wait. A man came up to me and said, 'The most unusual thing has happened. An orthopedic surgeon has heard about your situation—he's agreed to see you.' This surgeon became my doctor all the way through my healing. When I saw him, he looked so radiant and wonderful that I said, 'You look like an angel!'

"I told him I had called for prayers and right afterward I'd been told he would see me. He said, 'I don't know a lot about prayer, but yours must have worked!'

"The break healed very fast, and later he told me he'd never seen anybody heal so quickly in his life. But even though the break healed, my shoulder remained frozen. The doctors said that I would have to have surgery to fix it. I had an intuitive feeling that if I moved back to Unity and started praying with other people again, the shoulder would be healed. I came back to the prayer room. Amazingly, many of the calls I got were about arms and backs.

"One day I was sitting in the chapel talking with a man about Unity co-founder Myrtle Fillmore's prayers and healing. All of a sudden I could feel a tremendous energy surge inside of me, and later that day I could move my arm. The shoulder is healed now. I know without a doubt it was prayer that did it.

"Someone asked me, 'What would you do, where would you go, if you had all the money in the world?'

"I said, 'I'd be at Silent Unity.'"

Silent Unity can be reached at 816-246-5400. Those in financial need can call toll-free at 1-800-669-7729.

# Twelve

# A WHOLE LIFE HEALING

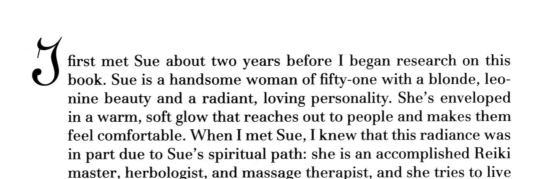

I first met Sue about two years before I began research on this book. Sue is a handsome woman of fifty-one with a blonde, leonine beauty and a radiant, loving personality. She's enveloped in a warm, soft glow that reaches out to people and makes them feel comfortable. When I met Sue, I knew that this radiance was in part due to Sue's spiritual path: she is an accomplished Reiki master, herbologist, and massage therapist, and she tries to live each day according to God's will.

What I didn't know until much later was that Sue's radiance also is a product of triumph over pain and trauma—so much pain and trauma that at times life to her had not been worth living, and Sue had attempted either to numb herself senseless or end life altogether through suicide.

For decades, Sue rode a hellish roller coaster of sexual and physical abuse, verbal abuse, substance abuse, failed marriages, failed jobs, low self-esteem, suicide attempts, and a death sentence from doctors who judged a physical ailment of hers to be terminal.

What kept her going was prayer and a faith in God. What enabled her to beat every single one of her problems and rise like a magnificent phoenix from her own ashes—was prayer. Today she can say, "I am the answer to my own prayers to God."

Throughout her life, Sue constantly prayed for deliverance from an onslaught of unhappiness. Her prayers were always answered, though sometimes God's answers were not what she wanted to hear.

Sue grew up in a country home environment that was anything but cozy and safe. From her earliest memories, she remembers her mother as an angry woman who took her emotions out on Sue and her brother. "You're a bad girl and nobody wants you," was the terrible message pounded over and over into Sue's sensitive heart. Sue's father was remote and passive, isolated from the family and oblivious to the abuse.

Sue's grandparents were also part of the abuse. Her grandmother once slammed Sue's arms down on a hot stove in order to teach her a lesson not to touch the stove; her arms were burned. And from the time Sue was five until she was eight, her grandfather sexually molested her.

The grandparents lived in a hotel that had no electricity. Whenever her parents went away, they left Sue and her older brother in the charge of the grandparents. Sleeping in dark rooms without electricity was scary for Sue. Her grandfather would tuck her and her brother away in separate rooms and then return to Sue's room to fondle her. It was preferable to being in the inky darkness alone, but it filled Sue with shameful, bad feelings. These experiences and feelings colored her relationships for years to come.

It was hard to stay afloat in these dark, treacherous pools. Luckily for Sue, her mother packed her and her brother off to a little country

Baptist church every Sunday alone. There, in Sunday school, Sue learned about Jesus and how he saved anyone who called upon him for help. She learned how to pray. And she prayed earnestly to be taken away from her fear-riddled home life.

Sudden, complete rescue did not come. Sue was not miraculously whisked away from home. Her salvation did come, but first she had to learn—over time and trial—that God does not banish our obstacles from our path, but helps us find our own ways to overcome them.

Though total rescue did not come, Sue's prayers were answered with relief. A relative who lived across the street took pity on Sue and began inviting her to spend more and more time in her home, with herself and her son. There, Sue basked, at least for periods, in peace, love, and attention.

As Sue matured, she began relating to males the only way she knew how, with precocious sexual behavior. She began having sexual relations with older men at an early age. Her underlying motive was a desperate attempt to find love. Instead, her sense of shame increased.

Sue was sixteen when she suffered a serious accident. A gas stove exploded in her face, severely burning her face and arms and burning off most of her hair. She escaped being permanently scarred, she believes, because her mother—who was a healer—defied a doctor's advice to administer yellow sulfur cream to the burned areas and did a healing on Sue.

But what she needed almost more than a physical healing was a healing of her soul. That need remained unfulfilled.

The burns left Sue in severe pain, which was too much for her to bear on top of her psychic pain. She fervently prayed to God, *Please let me die now, because I can't stand all this anymore.*

God's answer was no. Sue was devastated. She felt let down and betrayed. How could God leave her in such unbearable misery?

After her recovery, Sue attempted to escape her circumstance by marrying a man ten years older than she. She had a baby right away.

The infant filled her with a sense of purpose for the first time in her life. She was needed. And she was *loved*.

But having a child was no instant cure for a young lifetime full of pain and abuse. Deep inside, Sue still carried around a weighty baggage. Years later, she would liken it to walking around with her belly full of pus.

By age eighteen, Sue had a second child, but it died in infancy as the result of an underdeveloped lung. At about the same time, she confronted the horror that her marriage was failing.

This time, instead of asking God to let her die, Sue decided to take matters into her own hands. She asked her mother to take her little son with her for the day. While they were gone, Sue went to her mother's refrigerator, where she knew she would find a quantity of prescription drugs that her mother always kept on hand. Sue consumed enough pills, she thought, to kill herself.

The attempt might have succeeded, had Sue's mother not telephoned. Getting no answer, her mother became worried and returned to the house, to find Sue sprawled on the bed unconscious. An ambulance was summoned. Sue regained consciousness enough to remember only that her son was crawling over the bed bawling her name as she was lifted up by the medical team.

Sue spent six weeks hospitalized in a psychiatric ward. As soon as she was released, she sliced her wrists. It was more a pitiful cry for help than a serious attempt to end her life. Her mother sent her off to live with relatives.

Sue got a divorce and married a second time. She returned to school and earned a GED, then went to college and graduated to work as a dietary manager in a nursing home. On the surface, it may have appeared to others that she was finally on top of things. But Sue's heart was still a Pandora's box of unresolved pain and shame. Over the next decade, she submerged herself in alcohol and drugs.

"I did that for relief," she said, recounting her experiences to me.

"They helped me cope with the pain that I was feeling all the time. Heroin was the only thing that I didn't touch. I did LSD, I did cocaine, I did alcohol. How did I manage to function? Let me tell you how I functioned. I was in so much emotional pain that it took a tremendous amount of drugs and alcohol just to numb me out. I smoked as much as twenty-six marijuana cigarettes a day. I took prescriptions of Librium or Valium on top of that. I drank two six-packs of beer every night. It took *that much* for me to be able to live with me. That's how much emotional pain I was in. I was still walking around with a ball of pus in my belly. It all started with the sexual abuse as a child. Through the years, I did a lot of ugly things trying to find love. Looking for love in all the wrong places, you know? People, places, things, food, sex— whatever it was, *something* had to make me feel better. I think when you're abused early on in life, it's hard to want to live, because you feel so dirty. You struggle to live."

And struggle to live Sue did. During those troubled years, she tried five more times to kill herself, usually through drug overdoses.

Through it all, prayer remained an anchor. Sue's second husband was Catholic, and she began attending the Catholic church. She had her son baptized a Catholic. When the second marriage was over after twelve years, Sue converted to Catholicism herself.

She quickly remarried for a third time. This relationship lasted a scant two years, shattered by Sue's discovery of his involvement in an extramarital sexual relationship. She found him in bed at home with another woman. To make matters more bizarre, ensconced in bed in another room in the house was the woman's husband and the couple's young daughter.

"I went up to my husband, pulled him by the hair on his head and said, 'Get up and act like a gentleman in your own house!'" Sue recalled. "My husband got up and beat the crap out of me. I just went crazy. My mind literally blanked out. All I did afterward was sit and droop over a coffee table."

Sue ended the marriage. It was 1976 and she was thirty-three. "I began to really look at my life and kept praying for help," she said. "I asked God to help me to be a better person, to be different. I felt my prayers weren't being answered. I was a miserable, negative person, and I felt sorry for myself a lot. I was on a constant pity party. I attracted negative people."

Sue sought psychiatric help. She had a desire to change, but it was not strong enough to overcome her dependence on alcohol and drugs. She still had to hit bottom before her prayers would be answered, and Sue would find the strength to turn her life around.

After her divorce from her third husband, Sue took a roommate in to share her house. Carol (not her real name) was fresh out of a drug rehabilitation program, but soon drifted back to drugs and drink. "We enabled each other to drink and maintain a household," Sue said. "The outside world never knew we were drunk. The outside world thought we were just two businesswomen, and I had my son, who was growing up. Things looked okay to the outside world, but actually they were awful."

Together, they decided to try and stop their substance abuse. Carol was Catholic, and so they agreed to go to mass every day and pray to God to help them stop their destructive behavior.

"It took six months, but this is how God answered my prayer," said Sue. "He knew me well enough to know that it would take some crisis or devastating blow to me for me to stop. I'd gone out drinking with another friend of mine. I came back to find Carol really angry at me for not calling to let her know where I was.

"I don't remember what happened next, because I was in a blackout until the next morning. I got up and all I saw was blood on the wall. Carol was gone. I called her office and was told that she was in the hospital. It took a couple days for me to find out that I had—according to Carol—broken both her jaws and that I had beat her up. She said I had come home and gotten mad. Alcoholism can turn you into a nightmare in a New York second. I had had previous episodes of alcoholic violence sporadically throughout my life.

"I was devastated! I called my son and I asked him to please come and take me to an AA meeting, and he did. That was eleven years ago, and I have not had a drink or drug since.

"So God did answer my prayers. I prayed to stop drinking, and he knew me well enough to know what it would take to answer my prayer. God puts in our life what we need, when we need it, and I think that He will give us exactly what we're praying for. It took me two years in AA to be able to forgive the past and turn my life around—and to find out that I had not broken Carol's jaw in the manner that she described. I was just so drunk that I fell on her, and her jaw was crushed in the process.

"Through the last eleven years, I've learned not to pray for anything specific, but to pray to ask God to put in my life what I need and the wisdom to carry it out. And that's exactly what I do. I try to live for the day. God gave me back a life. Rather, he gave me a life that I had never had. Hope began to come into my life, which I had never had."

Turning her life around was in itself a painful experience. "For the first six years of my sobriety," said Sue, "I was numb, and all I had was prayer."

Sue learned massage. She wanted to go into massage practice but was afraid to let go of her job. She prayed to God for advice. The answer came when she lost her job at a hospital due to a change in ownership. She took another job—and was fired from it. She took still a third job and was fired from that too. "I had no choice but to go into practice," said Sue. "Here again, God answered my prayer. God has never failed me. People are there for you as much as they can be, but they have their own worlds. If you allow God to do so, he will truly work in your life.

"The next thing I know, I'm working two part-time jobs and selling vacuum cleaners and trying to get my practice together. Within six months, I had a full-time practice. That was God working in my life. I didn't advertise; I didn't do anything. It was all word-of-mouth. That's one of God's little miracles that he shows you—or a big miracle for me, because it was my support. I barely had a way of making it, had no health insurance, no house insurance. My insurance agent called his underwriters and said I had a massage parlor, and they canceled me the next day.

"So for a year, it was me and God! The only thing I could do without getting bogged down in fear was to turn everything over to God, and say, 'God, you've got to keep me healthy, and please don't let anything happen to the house.' Then I had to let go of it. That's all I could do. I kept in my mind that God would take care of it if I let go."

Subsequently, Sue learned Reiki (she is now a Reiki master), herbology, and hypnotherapy, all of which furthered her on her spiritual path. "I began filling the hole in my soul with God—developing the God from within me," she explained. "That's the still, quiet voice within.

"Every night, I thank God for everything that has happened during my day," Sue said. "Not just the good things, but the things that feel uncomfortable. There are no bad things in my life today, only things that feel uncomfortable. Those keep me on my path—that spiritual path of becoming more like God, keeping the soul clean.

"I talk to God throughout the whole day," she went on. "I know the days when I'm in charge, and the days when God is in charge. There are some days I start all over again by backing up and saying, 'God, please show me the direction to go.'

"I've come so far! I've gone through many addictions: alcohol, drugs, sex, money, cigarettes, sugar, caffeine. Now I'm working on my weight. I've come from hell to happiness, or comfortability, anyway. I'm not sure I know what happiness is, but I do know what being comfortable in life is: not feeling miserable; being open to change; having hope in my life; knowing that things can happen; having manageability in my life."

"How has your relationship with God changed over all of this?" I asked.

"When I was growing up, I thought God was a being, a man, who lived in heaven, and who I had to fear, because he would punish me for being a bad person. The God of my present understanding is that he is a gentle, loving God. I believe that God is in everything and every-one—everything I touch, everything I see, everything I smell, every-thing I hear. God is all of my senses. I think God works through everything—people, places, and things. My God is a loving God. He will continue to offer me the best, and I believe that if we allow ourselves to be filled with God, then we attract God-like people and God-like things into our life."

I asked Sue what her experiences had taught her about prayer.

"I used to pray for things," she said. "Like, I used to pray for money. But everything has a price. I've learned instead to pray for God to put in my life what I need, when I need it, and to grant me the wisdom and the courage to carry it through. When I do that, I always feel so much better about me and about life, because life just flows. It's like an energy that comes through, and it moves!"

"What do you say to people who feel their prayers aren't being answered?"

"That it's not time for the prayers to be answered yet," Sue said without hesitation. "That things are not in place. God has to work through this material world. I'm not saying that he can't instantly change things, because that's what miracles are all about. If you're ask-ing God for something, he's going to put the perfect condition in your life. So you have to wait for that perfect condition to be there. I say to many people, things aren't over until they're over, and things aren't ready until they're ready. The time may not be right yet. Keep praying. Or, I suggest that they need to let go of the outcome. Give God the time to work it out. Our time and God's time are not the same. That's often a hard one for us, because we get impatient and want results right away.

"Sometimes the answer is no," Sue went on, "as I know so well from my own experience. That's a hard one too. Sometimes God loves us enough just to tell us no, because we don't know ourselves and what our wants and needs are. We only know what we *think* we want.

"A lot of times we get what we think we want and we're sorry we have it, because we don't know how to handle it. I hear a lot of stories like that in my practice.

"I have been through a catastrophic illness myself. About ten years ago, I had chronic obstructive pulmonary disease, a result of smoking. Doctors gave me five years to live. I went around with a tube up my nose and a little oxygen pack on my back. I hooked the tube up to a portable oxygen machine. I couldn't breathe without oxygen twenty-four hours a day, seven days a week. I went to work with the tube. I had frequent bouts of pneumonia and chronic bronchitis. I prayed to God to put the things in my life that would heal me. I got a healing, all right! The message was, 'Stop smoking, Sue!' The message also was, 'Don't be so afraid of taking life in!' You see, I wasn't breathing all the way deep into my lungs. Symbolically, I wasn't 'breathing in' life as deeply as I could, because of fear.

"I just seemed to be chronically ill. I remember being in the hospital, oxygen tubes up my nose, skin gray, very ill, addicted to cigarettes so bad that I'd sneak into the bathroom—I could hardly crawl out of the bed, but I'd take the oxygen off and sneak into the bathroom to smoke, and then I could hardly make it back to the bed. I was a sick, sick person, mentally, physically, and spiritually. I just lay there in bed and knew I could choose to die.

"Early one morning, about four-thirty, I looked out my window and had a vision—I saw what I thought was Bethlehem. It was just absolutely fantastic! I saw these wonderful buildings and this wonderful light. It was heaven. I don't particularly equate Bethlehem with heaven, but that's what I saw and felt.

"Somehow I knew that I could die at that point. I thought, 'God, it's up to you. If I'm to stay here, put in my life what I need to remain.'

"I closed my eyes, and when I woke up, I was still alive. That was God's answer. Just like when I was a teenager and prayed to die, this answer devastated me. But that's what I had to work with. And so I decided I had to buckle down and do some hard work on myself, to allow the spirit of God to flow into me."

Sue gave up smoking and is recovering from her respiratory illness. She rarely needs oxygen and maintains an active schedule.

"Today, there is *real* life in me. I'm living life on life's terms, which is not always so great. But I'm not faking it, I'm not pretending, I'm not pacifying anybody. I'm living each day and each moment as they come. I think that's all any of us really has. We don't have yesterday, we don't have tomorrow, we have right now."

# Thirteen

## Prayer and the Modern Mystic

Throughout history, mysticism has been a road less traveled, calling only to adepts who have been willing to give up everyday life for austere circumstances in order to harken only to the divine. Today, increasingly, mysticism calls ordinary people in all walks of life, who manage to follow the path while maintaining mainstream lives.

The mystical path is nonetheless a demanding one. The mystic must over and over again surrender, surrender, surrender his or her selfhood to God. In mysticism, the deepest mysteries of God are explored through prayer and meditation. In mysticism, one attains the highest form of prayer, which is resting in the Silence in union with God. It is a reality beyond rational thought, a movement of mind and soul into the Source of all Being, a state in which there are no words, images, symbols, or self-awareness.

The theologian Rudolf Otto defined mysticism by method:

the mysticism of introspection and the mysticism of unifying vision. In introspection, the mystic turns inward in contemplation and meditation, withdrawing from the external world and finding within the depths of the soul the One. In the unifying vision, which Otto also called the Way of Unity, the mystic looks outward to the world to find the One. Most modern mystics prefer the path of introspection.

"Prayer elevates us to cosmic levels," says Rev. Richard L. Batzler. "When we enter into prayer, we come into an awareness of ourselves as spiritual beings. We come into an awareness of God. Awareness is one of the first steps in the mystical process. The highest knowledge you can have is to know that God is beyond all of our knowing."[1]

The decision to embark on the Mystic Way takes one through a series of psychological stages. Evelyn Underhill, in her classic study, *Mysticism* (1955), defined five of these, though not all may be experienced by any one mystic. The path itself is characterized by a vacillation between states of intense pleasure and intense pain. The five stages are:

1. *The Awakening of the Self* to consciousness of Divine Reality. Typically, this is a well-defined, often sudden experience and is characterized by great joy.
2. *The Purgation of the Self.* The mystic, through discipline and/or mortification, attempts to rid himself of imperfections and material desires, which are obstacles to unity.
3. *Illumination.* A happy state of apprehension of the Divine Presence, experienced in contemplation and meditation. It is not true union. Many mystics never get beyond Illumination. Artists and highly creative persons tend to have Illumination experiences.
4. *The Purification of the Self.* Also called the "Dark Night of the Soul." The mystic attempts total surrender of Self, personal identity, and will to the Divine and is plunged into a painful and unhappy state of the absence of the Divine Presence.

5. *Union with the One.* The mystic achieves a permanent and transcendent level of reality.

Underhill states, "As the Mystic Way involves transcendence of character, the sublimation of the instinctive life, and involvement of the whole man to higher levels of vitality, his attainment of freedom; so the ascent of the ladder of contemplation involves such as transcendence, or movement to high levels of liberty, of his perceptive powers."[2]

The steps on this ladder to higher consciousness, to union with God, have been called by Christian mystics degrees of prayer or orison. Mystical prayer is not a petition to God for any desired thing, even for union itself. Rather, it is formless, a yearning of the soul. Mystical prayer flourishes in the fertile soil of the Silence. Tremendous healing can take place through mystical prayer; first, on the level of the soul. Healing must occur here before it can occur on lower levels of consciousness and manifest in the mundane world as emotional, physical, psychological, or mental healing.

In Christian mysticism, the degrees of prayer are a process of deepening introversion. Various terms have been used to describe these degrees, or stages. According to Underhill, the beginning is Recollection. This is not remembrance, as the term suggests, but rather a meditative state involving the focusing of concentration. This breaks the connection to the outer world and what Underhill calls the "Eye of Time"—which is awareness of external phenomena—and facilitates the drift of consciousness into a subliminal, intuitive state. In Eastern meditation, this is often accomplished through the repetition of a mantra, a sacred word or phrase. In Christian mysticism, the pray-er begins Recollection by setting the mind on a name or attribute of God, a small piece of Scripture, an incident in the life of Christ, or some other religious event. These create a mental field that pushes the mundane world out of awareness. In Recollection there remains a clear separation between Self and the Other—God remains transcendent rather than immanent.

The next great stage of mystical prayer is the Quiet, also called the Silence. Consciousness sinks into the Infinite, and there is a steady withdrawal of the senses. Yet, awareness of the pray-er's personality remains. The Quiet, says Underhill, marks the transition from "natural" prayer to "supernatural" prayer, in which all symbols and images of mundane reality begin to disappear. It is a psychic state of total humility and receptivity.

The prayer of Quiet was stressed by all the great medieval Christian mystics, who considered it essential to contemplation. Meister Eckhart, who wrote enthusiastically about it, called it "the New Birth" and "that immobility by which all things are moved." St. John of the Cross called it the "interior silence" and said it is the place where God "secretly annoints the soul and heals our deepest wounds."

From the Quiet, the pray-er enters the state of Contemplation, which is a general term that covers various states of consciousness. There may be raptures, inner visions, and voices; feelings of peace and bliss; and, in highest form, union with God.

Ambrose Worrall believed prayers of meditation and contemplation, which have no words, images, or ideas, to be important to spiritual healing. Such prayers, he said, serve to "open the doors to spiritual knowledge to turn on the healing current, and to bring into focus that which is ready to reveal through the use of spiritual gifts."[3]

## St. Teresa of Avila

One of the greatest Christian mystics—and one of the greatest authorities on mystical prayer—is St. Teresa of Avila (1515–1582), the Carmelite nun and founder of the Discalced Carmelite Order, a reform movement. ("Discalced" means they wore no shoes.) More than four hundred years after her passing, her writings on prayer continue to set a standard, not only for mystics, but for anyone interested in fruitful prayer.

She was born Teresa de Cepeda y Ahumada to a noble family on March 28, 1515, in or near Avila in Castille. Her mother died when she was fifteen, which upset her so much that her father sent her to an Augustinian convent in Avila. Her exposure to the monastic life convinced her she wanted to become a nun, but her father forbade it as long as he was living. At about age twenty or twenty-one, she left home secretly and entered the Incarnation of the Carmelite nuns in Avila. Her father dropped his opposition.

In 1538, soon after taking the habit, Teresa began to suffer from ill health, which she attributed to the change in her life and diet. It was through her chronic and severe afflictions that Teresa discovered the power of prayer, which enabled her to heal herself and which then became the focus of her spiritual life and her writings.

In her autobiography, *Life,* Teresa comments on her "many ailments" during her first year in the convent, including increasingly frequent fainting fits and heart pains so severe that others became alarmed. She was often semiconscious or unconscious altogether. She opined that these problems were sent by God, who was offended at her innate "wickedness." Some experts believe she suffered from malaria.

Her father attempted to help her by packing her off to a town, Becedas, which had a great healing reputation. There she stayed for nearly a year, but failed to improve. She was given experimental cures by a woman healer. She described the remedies as "so drastic I do not know how I endured them. . . . So strong were the medicines that after two months I was almost dead, and the pains in my heart, of which I had come to be cured, were so much more intense that I sometimes felt as if sharp teeth were being plunged into it. I was in such agony that they feared I might go mad. I had lost a great deal of strength, for I felt such a loathing for food that all I could take was a little liquid;

and I had a continuous fever. I was reduced by the daily purges that had been given for almost a month, and so shrivelled that my nerves began to contract, giving me such unbearable pain that I could get no rest by night or day, and fell into a state of great misery."[4]

The trip to this healing center was fortuitous, however, because en route Teresa visited an uncle, who gave her a book entitled *The Third Alphabet,* which contained lessons in the prayer of recollection (introspection). Teresa was so delighted with the book that she began to use it as her guide in prayer, and it served as her primary guide for the next twenty years.

Her failure to improve under the medicinal administrations given her caused her father to bring Teresa back home. There she deteriorated badly over several months, and finally she fell into a deathlike coma for three days. The Sacrament of Extreme Unction was given to her in expectation of her imminent death. For a day and a half, a grave was left open for her at her convent, and rites for the dead were performed at a Carmelite friary nearby. Teresa made a complete confession, but instead of dying, she began to recover. She wrote:

> After my four days of insensibility, I was in such a state that only the Lord knows the unbearable torments I suffered. My tongue was bitten to pieces, and my throat was so choked from having eaten no food and from my great weakness, that I could not even swallow water. My bones seemed to be wrenched out of their sockets, and there was a great confusion in my head. As a result of all those days of torture I was all twisted into a knot, and unless someone moved them for me, I could not more move arm, foot, hand, or head than if I had been dead. All that I could move, I think, was one finger of my right hand. It was impossible for anyone to see me, for I was in such pain all over that I could not bear it. They used to move me in a sheet, one taking one end and one the other; and this state of things lasted till Palm Sunday. My sole relief was that so long as I was not touched my pains often ceased, and then when I had had a little rest I considered myself well. I was afraid that my patience would

fail, and so I was extremely pleased when I found myself free from these sharp and continuous pains, even though the cold fits from an intermittent fever from which I still suffered remained almost unendurably severe. I continued to have a great distaste for food.[5]

So, instead of receiving a corpse, her convent received her corpse-like body. Teresa remained in this state for eight months, paralyzed. Gradually, the paralysis improved—she began to crawl around on her hands and knees—but it continued in some form for three years. Teresa said that her sole anxiety was to get well so that she could pray in solitude. Through daily mental prayers, she healed herself over a long and slow recovery. She attributed her return to health to St. Joseph, who had come to the aid of Mary, mother of Jesus, during their times of trial when Jesus was an infant. It took her three years to recover the ability to walk. It was not until she reached the age of forty that the principal symptoms of her illness finally and entirely disappeared.

During those years of slow recovery, Teresa struggled with her spiritual life and described her prayer life as unpleasant. "I don't know what heavy penance could have come to mind that frequently I would not have gladly undertaken rather than recollect myself in the practice of prayer,"[6] she said.

Throughout her monastic life, Teresa did not seek out these experiences, but resigned herself to God's will and considered them a divine blessing. She spent long periods in the prayer of quiet and the prayer of union, during which she often fell into a trance and at times entered into mystical flights in which she felt as though her soul were lifted out of her body. She likened ecstasy to a "delectable death," saying that the soul becomes awake to God as never before when the faculties and senses are "dead."

Once she complained to God in prayer about her sufferings. His answer came to her: "Teresa, so do I treat my friends!" She understood it to mean that there was purification in her suffering, but she nonetheless had the pluck to retort, "That's why you have so few [friends]!"

Teresa exhorted others to prayer and especially to passive, mental prayer (though she continued to do both vocal and mental prayer throughout the rest of her life). However, she did believe that vocal prayer required mental prayer in order to be effective.

Prayer, she said, was the door to "those very great favours" that God then conferred on her, in the form of intellectual visions (formless, neither external nor internal), raptures, ecstasies, being engulfed in the presence of God, and—most important—union.

"In the twenty-seven years that I have practiced prayer," she wrote, "ill though I have trodden the road and often though I have stumbled, His Majesty has granted me experiences for which others need thirty-seven, or even forty-seven, although they may have progressed in penitence and constant virtue."[7]

Teresa likened prayer to the cultivation of a garden. She outlined four steps for the watering of the garden so that it would produce fruits and flowers, which are the measure of the pray-er's progress in love. These steps can be followed by beginners and adepts alike.

The first, and simplest, step is meditation, which Teresa said is like drawing water from a deep well by hand, in that it is slow and laborious.

The second step is through quiet, in which the senses are stilled and the soul can then receive some guidance; thus, the pray-er gets more water for the energy expended. The soul begins to lose its desire for earthly things.

The third step is through the prayer of union, in which there is contact between the pray-er and God, and there is no stress. The garden, in fact, seems to be self-watered as though from a spring or a little stream running through it. Teresa confessed that she had little understanding herself of this step. The senses and mental faculties, she said, could occupy themselves only and wholly with God.

The fourth step is done by God himself, raining water upon the garden drop by drop. The pray-er is in a state of perfect receptivity, loving trust, and passive contemplation. Physically, the pray-er faints away into a kind of swoon, Teresa said; her description resembles the trance states described by many mystics of many faiths.

Teresa often came out of deep prayer states finding herself drenched in tears. These were tears of joy, she attested. Mystics in modern times also experience this.

She made such rapid progress in her prayer that she was concerned that she was being deceived by the devil, because she could not resist the favors when they came, nor could she summon them—they came spontaneously. Also, she considered herself to be a weak and wicked person. Nonetheless, she was granted many prayers of silence and union, some of which lasted for long periods of time.

Teresa sought out spiritual counsel in an attempt to allay her fears. Some of her advisers could not believe that such favors could be experienced by a weak woman and fueled her fears of devilish interference. One more objective adviser told her to put the matter before God by reciting the hymn *Veni, Creator* as a prayer. This she did for the better part of a day, at which point a rapture came over her that was so strong it nearly carried her away. She said, "This was the first time that the Lord had granted me this grace of ecstasy, and I heard these words: 'I want you to converse now not with men but with angels.' This absolutely amazed me, for my soul was greatly moved and these words were spoken to me in the depths of the spirit. They made me afraid therefore, though on the other hand they brought me much comfort, after the fear—which seems to have been caused by the novelty of the experience—had departed."[8]

In 1562, despite opposition, Teresa founded a convent in Avila with stricter rules than those that prevailed at Carmelite monasteries. She sought to establish a small community that would follow the Carmelite contemplative life, in particular unceasing prayer. In 1567 she was permitted to establish other convents and went on to found sixteen others. She dedicated herself to reforming the Carmelite order. At age fifty-three, she met the twenty-six-year-old John Yepes (later known as St. John of the Cross), who worked to reform the male Carmelite monasteries. After a period of turbulence within the Carmelites from 1575–1580 the Discalced Reform was recognized as separate.

By 1582 Teresa had founded her seventeenth monastery, at Burgos. Her health was broken, and she decided to return to Avila. The rough journey proved to be too much, and upon arriving at the convent, Teresa went straight to her deathbed. Three days later, On October 4, 1582, she died. The next day, the Gregorian calendar went into effect, dropping ten days and making her death on October 14. Her feast day is October 15. Teresa was canonized in 1662 by Pope Gregory XV and was declared a Doctor of the Church—the first woman so honored—in 1970 by Pope Paul VI.

During Teresa's travels throughout Spain on her reform mission, she wrote a number of books, some of which have become spiritual classics. The first of those was *Life,* her autobiography, written in 1565. On November 18, 1572, Teresa experienced a spiritual marriage with Christ as bridegroom to the soul. Two of the fruits of that marriage were *The Way of Perfection* (1573), about the life of prayer, and *The Interior Castle* (1577), her best-known work, in which she presents a spiritual doctrine, using a castle as the symbol of the interior life. The latter book was revealed to her in a vision on the eve of Trinity Sunday, 1577, in which she saw a crystal globe like a castle that had seven rooms; the seventh, in the center, held the King of Glory. One approached the center, which represents the Union with God, by going through the other rooms of Humility, Practice of Prayer, Meditation, Quiet, Illumination, and Dark Night. She often referred to Christ as the "heavenly bridegroom," but her later visions became less erotic and more religious in character.

Teresa's literary method of linking images has recently been found to be much more intricate and extensive than previously thought. Recent studies have found a timelessness to her writings and elements of feminist spirituality. Her words continue to inspire modern audiences. She once said to her followers, "I will give you a living book." She kept her promise.

## A modern mystic's path

Jim Rosemergy is a modern-day mystic—one of the "monks of the city," as he calls contemporary people who tread the Mystic Way. Jim was ordained as a Unity minister in 1976. He served at the founders' church, Unity on the Plaza, and worked for twelve years as a field minister, first in Raleigh, North Carolina, and then in Spokane, Washington. He is now an executive vice president of the Unity School of Christianity in Unity Village, Missouri. Prior to taking the spiritual road, Jim served in the U.S. Navy as an aviator and saw action in Vietnam.

Jim and his wife, Nancy, have long been students of the mystical path. In 1986 Jim received divine inspiration for what became his book, *Living the Mystical Life Today.* It was also revealed to him that modern "people of the earth are now ready to live the simple life of prayer and humility"; in other words, people are ready for the Mystic Way. Jim and Nancy founded Inner Journey, a nonprofit organization based in Lee's Summit, Missouri, that publishes books, educational materials and a quarterly newsletter, all devoted to mystical prayer. The purpose of Inner Journey is "to quicken and foster humankind's natural inclination to discover the truth of being," and it is committed to a life of prayer—"to let a consciousness of God be the beginning of every thought, feeling, and action."

Jim is the author of several other books; among them are *A Closer Walk with God,* which is a practical book on living a life of prayer, how to work in prayer groups, and how to follow a forty-day guide to a life of prayer; and *Even Mystics Have Bills to Pay.* The title of the latter one gave me a chuckle. Modern-day mystics can ill afford to retire to a cave or monastery; if they're going to survive in a tough world as well as further their spirituality, they've got to find ways to pay the mortgage, put food on the table, and put kids through college. The whimsical title, however, belies the practical and serious contents. *Even Mystics Have Bills to Pay* concerns the preparing of humanity for a new spirituality—beyond any religious dogma or creed—in the new millennium.

Like many who have worked with prayer and meditation for a long period of time, Jim has found that his understanding of prayer has shifted with experience and insight. Prayer is an important force in his life, and once it dramatically helped him heal himself of partial blindness in one eye.

"Prayer is an experience of the Presence," Jim told me in an interview. "It helps us to practice God's presence in everything that we do. Life is a consciousness of God.

"What prayer creates is deferred action. We don't act until we have an attunement to Spirit. Then the healing takes place. Healing can take many forms, even just becoming more sensitive to opportunities for growth, prosperity, and harmonizing relationships. That power is there for us on a daily basis, but often we don't recognize it. With prayer we are sensitized, and we begin to see events in different ways. Prayer opens us up and changes our lives."

Jim describe the experience in which prayer helped him heal his partial blindness. "I came to the ministry from the military. As you can well imagine, crying—or any show of emotion—is not the thing to do in the military. But when I arrived at Unity and my spiritual awakening began, I started to open up internally. I cried and cried at what I considered to be the most inopportune times. At first, I didn't like what was happening to me, but I couldn't close the floodgates once they were opened. I had to learn to accept my feelings. That acceptance, and a continued commitment to prayer, have helped me to develop a greater sensitivity to both people and to Spirit.

"I'm not embarrassed anymore to cry in public. If I'm overwhelmed, then that's how I feel. But back in the earlier days, I was self-conscious and tried to hold back the tears in front of others. On this one occasion, I was so moved emotionally that I wanted to cry, but I held it back. It was such a strain that I broke a blood vessel in the back of my left eye. I didn't know at the time what had happened. Then I noticed that at dead center of my left eye was a gray spot in my vision.

"I went to a doctor and he wanted to use a laser to seal the blood vessels that had burst. The problem was, that would have left a permanent blind spot, albeit smaller than the one I had. I told him I didn't want to do that. Instead, I worked with prayer and meditation, affirming that I was seeing with the eyes of spirit. It was healed, by the time I was into my second year in the ministerial school. I have no blind spot now at all.

"That was at a time in my life when I had more emphasis on physical healing," Jim said. "If that happened to me now, my approach would be different. I wouldn't emphasize healing my body or my eye, but instead I would invite spirit to use the situation to reveal to me my wholeness, the quality of my spirit.

"If we become conscious of our wholeness, then that consciousness will manifest itself, often as a healed body, but not always. In healing, it's hard to know just what is healed, and what does the individual need. For instance, take Helen Keller. If she had been healed of her blindness and deafness, humanity would have lost a great blessing. She taught us much about wholeness of spirit. The same principle applies to prosperity. Most people tend to look at prosperity as a certain amount of money or a job. I call prosperity the no-need state, in which we have whatever we need in order to be free of need. This sense of spiritual wholeness is the state of consciousness in which we feel God's presence."

Jim explained that when we pray to change something by enlisting God's aid, we are really recognizing that there are two powers: the power of God and the "power" of illness, evil, whatever. This creates resistance and conflict in prayer life. It is preferable to pray recognizing one power, God, and our oneness, or wholeness, with it. "I am one with God" or "I and the Father are one" are examples of affirmative prayers toward wholeness.

"In recent years, two affirmations have emerged from my prayer life," Jim said. " 'God is enough' and 'God is mystery.' These have generated literally hours of contemplation and meditation.

"When I pray for other people, I try not to bring into my consciousness the thoughts of the individual, or their name or their problem, because I think in God that problem is not present. I open myself to the experience of the Presence, the wonder. That's where the mystery comes in."

In the spring of 1992 Inner Journey conducted its first prayer experiment, called Fruits of Spirit, and aimed at deepening one's relationship with Spirit. Ninety people committed themselves to participating, and fifty people reported their results. When the reports were analyzed and tabulated, the Rosemergys were amazed at how quickly prayer bears fruit once a person commits to regular prayer, and also at the range of insights experienced. And, as pray-ers moved into the peace and relaxation that comes from meditative prayer, the willingness to pray was replaced by a desire to pray. Prayer was seen as necessary to life itself.

The twelve-week experiment began, appropriately, on Easter Sunday, April 19, and ended on July 11. The participants were asked to pray for twenty minutes every day. They were to keep in mind the fruits of Spirit that St. Paul wrote about in Galatians 5:22–23: "But the fruit of the Spirit is love, joy, peace, patience, kindness, goodness, faithfulness, gentleness, self-control: against such there is no law." In addition, participants were given two affirmations that expressed the essence of the experiment: *"Dear God, my friend, I am your tree of life. May I bear your fruits of love, joy, peace, patience, kindness, goodness, faithfulness, gentleness, and self-control."*

❌◼◗◼◗◼◗◼❌
PRAYER
AND THE
MODERN
MYSTIC
—
193

The participants prayed an average of six days a week, preferably in the morning. Busy schedules complicated this activity but pointed to how prayer requires simplicity and tends to simplify life in return.

Participants also reported having to deal with normal distractions, such as wandering minds, the tendency to fall asleep, the surfacing of negative emotions, anticipating results, and mentally rehashing the day. All these were useful in learning how to still the mind and let go. The Rosemergys point out that they are part of the normal process of learning how to pray, a process in which human consciousness is lifted to higher levels.

The Rosemergys call the first stage of this uplifting the High Meadow, a state of positive, joyful thoughts—but also of waiting. During this waiting, the mind wanders. Ideally, the pray-er strives to observe unconditionally this wandering and to be patient in the waiting. "The soul that waits walks with God," Jim said. "Waiting is challenging. We must keep a steady focus upon Spirit and give the gift of our attention to God."

Eventually, grace moves the pray-er to the next level, the Quiet. Here one releases self-awareness and awareness of one's surroundings and begins to move into awareness of God. "Inner healing takes place when we are in the Quiet," Jim told me.

Sometimes, instead of going into the Quiet, the pray-er goes into the Blessed State, in which divine inspiration and creativity pour into the senses and mind. Ideas and solutions to problems, and healings as well, spring forth in this state. There can be tremendous surges of energy and vitality as a result.

Beyond both the Quiet and the Blessed State is the Silence, in which self-awareness ceases—it is a state of total unconsciousness in which the senses and mental faculties are asleep. Here, we attain union with God. The Silence can be a fleeting experience of just a few moments—in fact, minutes of the Silence would have to be described as a trance state.

"Silence is the most accurate description I know of prayer and the Presence," said Jim. "The encounter with God is pure silence—a silence that is not the absence of sound, but the presence of God.

"Most people who have experienced the Silence don't realize it, because moments of total unconsciousness are very short. We don't even know we were 'there' until we return."

Despite its momentary nature, attaining the Silence can change lives forever. Values shift, divine guidance comes, the pray-er returns to the mundane world with a new sense of mission and purpose in life, or fortified preparation for something that lies ahead.

Of the fruits of the prayer experiment, love was the one most often reported during the first week. Love was followed by peace, patience, and joy as the experiment went on. The initial encounter with God initiated a cleansing process, in which pray-ers found themselves letting go of past hurts and forgiving others and themselves. Anger and resentment are barriers to attaining the presence of God, said Jim, and it is essential to remove them.

Other fruits reported were self-control, gentleness, and kindness. Pray-ers also said they frequently experienced crying during and after prayer—the tears of joy shed by Jim and described by Teresa of Avila and other mystics.

Changes that the pray-ers observed in themselves included:

* Increased calm, patience, and tolerance, especially in stressful situations;
* Healing, cessation of need for blood pressure medicine, better dietary

habits, loss of weight, cessation of smoking, greater sense of physical well-being;

* Greater intuition, more self-awareness, receptivity to clear divine guidance, greater awareness of interior world;
* Greater ability to receive love and see beauty in others, even when they are not on their best behavior;
* Less judgmental and critical of self and others, increased trust, more forgiveness, acceptance of own mistakes, increased candor;
* Greater appreciation for beauty in the world;
* Improved performance on the job, greater prosperity, new ideas;
* Feeling of calm through major life-changes, such as divorce, new job, bankruptcy;
* Breaking up of old patterns;
* Increased closeness to God, focus on living in the moment.

It is interesting to note the insights the pray-ers experienced as they progressed through the weeks. The Rosemergys compiled the following in chronological order:

* Discovered or sensed a need to let go.
* Layers were being peeled away during prayer and meditation.
* More peace comes with letting go.
* My future depends upon the way I live today.
* Seek the Presence instead of worrying.
* I realized my purpose was to be conscious of Spirit.
* Fruits of Spirit are to be given away—shared.
* With faith in God, God will provide.
* "I showed up." (The Rosemergys comment that this was one of their favorite insights reported, for it shows the need to be persistent in prayer—to "show up" for prayer time without expectations.)
* Receiving love from others is not the way.
* I realized how much I needed the Quiet.

* In prayer and meditation, these words were heard: "Stop seeking me; realize my Presence."
* Another message: "No path trod, no search for God, my heart is His abode."
* As a result of prayer and meditation, I am better able to think about God while walking. I walk with God.
* Releasing prepares me for spiritual growth.
* There was a person in need. Rather than pray that the person be changed, I loved her.
* Nothing dramatic . . . it just works.
* Prayer is not something that happens. It takes practice.

It is evident that as the pray-ers got deeper into their prayer experience, the nature of their insights shifted from a focus on the self and day-to-day life, to a higher wisdom and sense of greater closeness to the divine.

## Centering prayer

A practical approach for attaining the interior stillness or Silence is the centering prayer, which focuses attention on the Presence. Centering prayer involves repeating a sacred word, but unlike mantra meditation, the focus is not on the word itself. Rather, the word—which can be something as simple as "love" or "peace"—serves to refocus the mind to silence when the mind begins to wander. A similar approach is used in Zen meditation. When thoughts intrude in Zen, one can count the breath up to ten or fifteen, starting over again as long as necessary to refocus the mind; or visualize an image of a pearl.

The word used in the centering prayer should be a word sacred to the pray-er, for it sets the intent of the prayer: to open one's self to the mystery of God.

As we can see from the experiences of Inner Journey, the Mystic Way is adaptable to the demands of modern life. It is not necessary to withdraw from the world in order to pursue the high road. In fact, the more we bring prayer into our lives, the more we center ourselves daily with prayer, the more we naturally follow the mystics' path.

The Mystic Way is one of the main avenues leading to a collective shift to higher consciousness, to a flowering of the Christ-consciousness within the soul. This shift has been foreseen by mystics and philosophers throughout centuries. As we shall see in the next chapter, the shift is already underway.

# Fourteen

# PRAYER POWER FOR THE NEW MILLENNIUM

In the previous chapters, we've focused on the healing power of prayer. We've seen how different kinds of prayer have worked for people in a range of situations.

But prayer is much more than stilling the mind and setting forces into motion. It is much more than support and a lifeline in daily life. Prayer is important to our future and our progress as human beings. *Prayer is a bridge to a new human being with a higher state of consciousness.* The evolutionary leap to this higher state is already underway.

## Evolution and consciousness

The upward-rising of human consciousness is not a new idea, though opinions have varied as to the speed and process of expansion. The origins of the idea can be found in the concept of the continuous evolution of all living things, which dates to classical times. Various Renaissance philosophers (and scientists as well), such as Spinoza and Kant, also embraced the idea of evolution. In the nineteenth century, Darwin made the theory of evolution famous. He posited that evolution takes place generation by generation through the process of natural selection, in which the fittest of a species survive and pass on their traits to succeeding generations.

However, the theory of evolution doesn't adequately explain what has happened and what is happening now. We have observed that throughout history, there has not been a steady pace of gradual change, but rather the species of the earth have experienced gradual change interspersed with evolutionary leaps. And, the rate of change is accelerating: witness what the human race has undergone in the past two hundred years alone, since the Industrial Revolution, versus changes over the past millennium.

The theory of evolution also doesn't adequately address changes in human consciousness, that mysterious quality or essence that distinguishes us from other types of life on earth. Consciousness embraces our thoughts, emotions, morals, ethics—and our apprehension of the Divine. Science has treated consciousness as an epiphenomenon of the brain—that is, something which does not exist outside the mind. However, research into alternative healing, altered states, psi, meditation, and prayer indicate that consciousness—even if we do not know precisely what it is—is nonlocal and functions outside of time and space. Science has yet to recognize what the mystic has known all along.

The French philosopher Henri Bergson conceived of the idea of "creative evolution," in which a mysterious "élan vital" pushes all living organisms toward their highest expression. This "élan vital" is only expressed fully in the human being.

Theologian, paleontologist, and philosopher Pierre Teilhard de Chardin was profoundly influenced by Bergson. Teilhard envisioned a grand picture of an evolving universe, in which cosmic evolution would take place in four phases: galactic, earth, life, and human. All of which depend on the integration of the psychic with the physical. Evolution implies the law of *complexification,* which means that as physical matter becomes more complex, so does consciousness, which is intrinsic to all life-forms. Thus the human race has arisen from, and is connected to, all other life-forms on earth, both physically and psychically. In its human form evolution becomes conscious of itself. The convergence of various human groups progressively will shape the ultrahuman, a process now underway. The ultimate goal is a convergence toward Christ, the "Omega point" at which human consciousness finds the ultimate integrity and unity. (In theological terms, this is the Christ-consciousness, or the Second Coming. The Second Coming can be seen, not as a literal event with the arrival of a Christ being, but as the unfolding of Christ-consciousness within the hearts and souls of all human beings.)

Teilhard used such phrases as *cosmogenesis,* for the development of a world with man at its center; *noosphere,* a collective human consciousness within the biosphere of the earth; *noogenesis,* for the growth of humankind's mind into a single, interthinking group; *hominization* and *ultra-hominization* for the future stages of man's transcendent humanization. The increasing numbers of humans and improving communications are fusing all parts of the noosphere together, Teilhard said. As a result, humankind will achieve more integrated and intense mental activity, which will facilitate the upward climb to higher stages of hominization.

Teilhard believed that the evolution of human consciousness would take place over thousands, perhaps even millions of years. Others, however, see the changes occurring at a much faster rate.

The mystic Sri Aurobindo (1872–1950) saw the development of a "Supermind" occurring over about two hundred years. The Supermind would be driven by spiritual development and would be the ultimate evolutionary product of Spirit. It would occur on both individual and collective levels.

❈❖❖❖❖❈
PRAYER
POWER FOR
THE NEW
MILLENNIUM
—
201

Gerald S. Hawkins, the British-American astronomer and mathematician famous for demonstrating that Stonehenge was an ancient observatory (*Stonehenge Decoded* [1965] and *Beyond Stonehenge* [1968]), has conceived of "mindsteps," or stages in the upward progress of the collective human mind. In his book *Mindsteps to the Cosmos* (1983), Hawkins likens mindsteps to a staircase, each step of which takes the collective mind further along in its understanding of the relation of humans to the cosmos. Mindsteps are not the same as paradigms or new worldviews, Hawkins says. Rather, they are examples of both but are more dramatic and are irreversible.

Mindsteps also are cumulative, building one on the other with some overlap. The changes in collective thinking wrought at each step depend on the accumulated growth at the previous level. For example, Copernicus's heliocentric discovery actually was put forward in 270 B.C. by Aristarchus—but the human collective simply wasn't ready for it, and Aristarchus was denounced for impiety by the Stoics. Even by Copernicus's time, heliocentrism still came as a tremendous shock.

Hawkins proposes five mindsteps, from 35,000 B.C. to the present time. Each successive step is shorter in duration, suggesting that we are heading through ever faster and faster changes in collective consciousness.

Mindstep 0, beginning in 35,000 B.C. and lasting for 32,000 years, was the Age of Chaos, in which the cosmos was seen, registered in the human mind, but left unexplained. Mindstep 1, beginning in 3,000 B.C. and lasting 3,150 years, ushered in the Age of Myth and Legend, in which the sun, moon, stars, and planets were explained by stories. It ended with the work of astronomer-mathematician Ptolemy.

Mindstep 2, beginning in 150 A.D. and lasting 1,393 years, was the Age of Order, which Copernicus brought to an end. Mindstep 3, beginning in 1543 and lasting 383 years, brought the Age of Revolution and the discoveries of science. Mindstep 4, beginning in 1926, heralded the Age of Space, our present mindstep.

By doing some calculations, Hawkins estimated that Mindstep 5 would arrive around 2021, followed by Mindsteps 6 and 7 in 2045 and 2051, respectively. Mindstep 5 might feature contact with extraterrestrials. Mindstep 6 might usher in an omega era called the Age of Spirit, which might see the development of time travel. Writes Hawkins, "Mindstep 6 could be proof, the demonstration of the existence of, something unseen, a new type of field connected with life, the existence of which is so persuasive that its general acceptance is inevitable. In religious contexts it could be identified with the world of the spirit. In this area there are scientific indicators which may or may not be precursors. There are the broad questions of telepathy, the existence or not of a vital force, the existence of the soul, and continuation of life after death. Then there are the unmeasurable human emotions of love, friendship, hate, pleasure, and pain. Are these all interlocking parts of a nonphysical cosmos?"

Hawkins's ideas about mindsteps were published ten years ago; we already seem to be in Mindstep 5, heading into Mindstep 6. We haven't had proof positive of extraterrestrial contact, as Hawkins mentioned might occur in Mindstep 5, although some would argue that contact has long been established. We are, however, pushing the edges of our collective consciousness into the nonphysical cosmos. We are more than shifting a paradigm; we are more than evolving. We are engaged in a consciousness *revolution* because of the nature and speed of the expansion of consciousness. We are not evolving new powers of consciousness but are reclaiming latent powers we've had all along but have not used over the millennia.

According to researcher and author John White, a new human being is in the process of emerging: *homo noeticus,* an advanced human being whose higher consciousness integrates mind, body and spirit, fostering a collective sense of identity, a sense of oneness, and motivations based on spiritual, rather than material, values. (*Noeticus* comes from the term "noetics," which is the study of consciousness.)

In Chapter 7, we saw that synchronicities increase the more a person prays or meditates. According to author and futurist Peter Russell, widespread occurrences of synchronicities can contribute to the emergence of a unitive level of consciousness:

> What we regard as curious chains of coincidences might likewise be the manifestation at the level of the individual of a higher organizing principle at the collective level, the as yet rudimentary social superorganism. As humanity becomes more integrated, functioning more and more as a healthy, high-synergy system, we might expect to see a steady increase in the number of supportive coincidences. A growing experience of synchronicity throughout the population could, therefore, be the first major indication of the emergence of a global level of organization.[1]

There are other reasons to pray regularly. A significant indication of the (r)evolution in consciousness is the apparent rise of "exceptional human experience" (EHE). This term was coined by parapsychologist Rhea A. White to embrace a wide range of phenomena, such as psi (which includes clairvoyance, clairaudience, telepathy, precognition, retrocognition, and psychokinesis); out-of-body experiences; near-death experiences (NDEs); apparitions; encounters with otherworldly beings such as angels, fairies, spirits, the Virgin Mary, etc.; encounters with UFOs and extraterrestrials; kundalini awakenings; and transcendent experiences in general such as quasi-mystical and mystical states of enlightenment and oneness. There have been no systematic studies of the incidence of all these experiences, but research literature on specific types of EHEs, such as the NDE, sightings of the Virgin Mary, and the kundalini awakening, indicate that more people are reporting such experiences.

Kenneth Ring, Ph.D., whose groundbreaking research of the NDE phenomenon was discussed in Chapter 10, sees NDEs as part of a collective "evolutionary thrust toward higher consciousness for humanity at large." Overwhelmingly, people who have an NDE are permanently transformed. Many experience:

* Physical changes, such as electromagnetic sensitivities and hypersensitivity to noise;
* Opened psychic and/or healing abilities;
* Loss of the fear of death;
* New or renewed sense of God, or Spirit, and the Oneness of all creation;
* Decrease in interest in material things and pursuits.

The NDE, suggests Ring, is one evolutionary mechanism that unlocks previously dormant spiritual potentials.

Another major bridge, one more closely related to prayer, is the kundalini awakening.

## Prayer and kundalini

Tangible and powerful energies are summoned and manifested by prayer. These energies can be hot and firelike or warm and soothing. A sensation of heat is one of the most common characteristics experienced in spiritual healing.

Intense firelike energy is characteristic of the kundalini force. "Kundalini" is a Sanskrit term meaning "snake." The name refers to a potent psycho-spiritual force often called "the serpent power." It is not a physical property that can be identified scientifically. In the yogic tradition it is the Self aware of its own divinity, of union with creation in a state of formlessness. Some of the kundalini literature describes it as the Great Goddess.

Kundalini resides dormant in the body in the chakra system. In yoga, the chakras (Sanskrit for "wheels") are whirlpool-like interfaces connecting the physical body to the etheric body—the vital envelope of energy also known as the aura. There are seven main chakras aligned along the spinal column. Each has a specific function. Generally, the chakras take in *prana,* or the universal life force, and transform it so that it can be used by the body. When kundalini is awakened, it can lead to a mystical experience and a permanently expanded higher state of consciousness. People who experience spontaneous awakenings of kundalini often find themselves changed as a result. Their psychic abilities open, and sometimes healing abilities appear as well.

Kundalini is often likened to fire, because it brings sensations of great heat, flames, and light. Some spiritual adepts learn how to raise this energy and control and direct it, such as for healing purposes.

The concept of kundalini is not limited to yoga. Mystical traditions around the world acknowledge this powerful energy by various names. Numerous Christian mystics throughout the centuries have described experiences—many brought on by long periods of intense prayer or contemplation—that parallel the descriptions of kundalini awakenings written by Eastern mystics. Among them are Meister Eckhart, St. Teresa of Avila, St. Catherine of Genoa, St. Catherine of Siena, St. John of the Cross, St. Paul, Pierre Teilhard de Chardin, Jacob Boehme, and Emmanuel Swedenborg. Rapture, levitation, ecstasy, illumination, surges of energy, oneness with God, visions, voices, inspirations, messages, and channeled writings are all part of the kundalini syndrome.

Like mystical experiences, kundalini awakenings can flood an individual with a sense of well-being, joy, and optimism. The ecstasy can reach such heights as to become almost unbearable torment and pain, as seen in the writings of the great Christian mystics.

Typical physical phenomena are:

*Decrease in bodily functions.* These include slowed breathing, pulse, circulation, and brain waves, as well as loss of awareness of one's body. In the state of rapture described by Christian mystics, the body seems to be on the verge of extinguishing. Teresa of Avila wrote in *The Interior Castle* that in the orison of union, the soul "is utterly dead to the things of the world and lives solely in God. . . . I do not even know whether in this state she has enough life left to breathe. It seems to me she has not; or at least that if she does breathe, she is unaware of it."

*Light.* One sees light, either exteriorized or internal, described as "illumination," "radiance," "lightning," "light of grace," and other terms. St. Paul may have had a kundalini awakening while on the road to Damascus. A brilliant light from heaven blinded him for three days, and he went without food and water. When his sight was restored, Paul was converted to Christianity. He ceased his persecutions of Christians and worked to spread the new religion. Within Islam, Muhammad, the founder of Islam, was awakened one night by an overpowering light, marking the first revelation to him of the Koran.

*Fire or psychosomatic heat.* Heat is a by-product of the enormous energy generated by some mystical experiences, especially in kundalini awakenings. Richard Rolle, the "father of English mysticism," experienced intense heat that manifested physically; he associated it with a fire of burning love.

*Paranormal powers.* As mentioned earlier, paranormal powers include levitation, telepathy, clairvoyance, materializations, haloes, stigmata, etc.

In recent years kundalini has been studied more by the Western world, particularly by psychotherapists, because kundalini awakenings can be traumatic. People can experience violent shaking, hypersensitivity to noise, insomnia, visions of gods and angels, travel to otherworldly realms, emotional swings, and other phenomena.

Nonetheless, researchers see tremendous potential in kundalini to transform human consciousness. The Kundalini Research Network, a coalition of professionals in various fields, formed in 1990, has defined kundalini as "the evolutionary/consciousness force. The awakening of kundalini in an individual effects a transformative process in the biological, psychological, and spiritual realms and results in a transformation of consciousness, and, ultimately, in the realization of the oneness of the individual and the universal consciousness. This transformation is a spiritual awakening that may occur in a continuum. The phenomena associated with the awakening of kundalini cannot be explained by any other known biological or physiological cause."

According to Bonnie Greenwell, a transpersonal psychotherapist in California, a founder of the Kundalini Research Network, and author of *Energies of Transformation,* kundalini "can be used to heal, transform, energize, and evolve higher levels of consciousness."

These are some of the very same results obtained through prayer. Prayer, like meditation, makes possible healing, spiritual transformation, increased creative energy, and a lifting up of consciousness to union with God. Prayer can activate kundalini. This activation is most demonstrable in group rituals but can come through solitary spiritual pursuits as well.

Kundalini is associated with enlightened states of consciousness that parallel the degrees of mystical prayer. A kundalini awakening can lead to samadhi, which is a superconscious state where the soul is united with God. Samadhi is the goal of all yogas. There are different levels of samadhi. The highest is complete union with God, or universal consciousness, which is beyond duality, time, space, and causality.

Many who have experienced and researched kundalini believe it to be an evolutionary energy, one that will increasingly manifest in more and more people as human consciousness evolves on an upward spiral. One of those persons was Gopi Krishna (1903–1984), an Indian civil servant whose writings on kundalini, based on his own experiences, are classics in the field. Krishna had what is probably one of the most dramatic cases of kundalini awakening on record.

Krishna meditated every morning for three hours for seventeen years. On Christmas Day in 1937 he had an explosive, roaring kundalini awakening of liquid light pouring up his spine and into his brain. He rocked and went out of his body enveloped in a halo of light. He felt his consciousness expand in all directions, and a vision of a silvery, lustrous light unfolded before him; he was like a small cork bobbing on the vast ocean of consciousness. This extraordinary experience happened once again, and then Krishna was plunged into 12 years of misery, during which he experienced a lot of physical pain and illness—due, he believed, to actual physiological changes caused by the surges of kundalini energy. In addition, he "experienced the indescribable ecstasies of the mystics . . . and the agonies of the mentally afflicted."

After twelve years, his body apparently adapted to the new energy and he stabilized, but he was permanently changed. Everything he saw appeared bathed in a silvery glow. He heard an inner cadence, called the "unstruck melody" in kundalini literature. Eventually, he was able to reexperience the bliss just by turning his attention inward. He became, he said, "a pool of consciousness always aglow with light." His creativity soared, and he wrote poetry and nonfiction books.

Krishna devoted much of the remainder of his life to learning everything he could about kundalini. He wrote seventeen books and numerous articles. He considered kundalini "the most jealously guarded secret in history" and "the guardian of human evolution." He believed it to be the driving force behind genius and inspiration. He also believed that the brain has within it the blueprint for mankind to evolve into a higher level of consciousness, one that will make use of kundalini. In educating others about it, Krishna told how it regenerates and restores the body and thus could be useful in discovering ways to improve health and lengthen life. He also suggested it could be useful in eradicating such conditions as mental retardation.

Krishna was keen to see kundalini awakening cultivated, especially in the West. Despite his conviction that it heralded a new threshold in human consciousness, he cautioned that the physical problems that accompany it could not be ignored. He observed that "any deep change in psychological state would be accompanied by change in the human organism and would be attended by subtle or even tangible changes in the brain and nervous system.''

R. M. Bucke, a Canadian psychiatrist who wrote the classic *Cosmic Consciousness* (1901), also believed kundalini to be of vital importance to the spiritual evolution of humanity.

Bucke's initial mystical experience came in a moment of dreamy, passive reverie. The experience involved fire imagery, but Bucke did not disclose whether he also felt heat. The experience, a vision that lasted but a few seconds, led him to investigate mystical experiences and write his book. The following description of Bucke's experience is given in the book's introduction:

> All at once, without warning of any kind, I found myself wrapped in a flame-colored cloud. For an instant I thought of fire, an immense conflagration somewhere close by in that great city; the next, I knew that the fire was within myself. Directly afterward there came upon me a sense of exultation, of immense joyousness accompanied or immediately followed by an intellectual illumination impossible to describe. Among other things, I did not merely come to believe, but I saw that the universe is not composed of dead matter but is, on the contrary, a living Presence; I became conscious in myself of eternal life.[2]

Bucke envisioned a ''revolutionizing of the human soul'' that would literally ''melt down'' all religions to a new religion that would exist the world over. Bucke wrote:

> An intellectual enlightenment of illumination which alone would place the individual on a new plane of existence—would make him almost a member of a new species. To this is added a state of moral exaltation, an indescribable feeling of elevation, elation, and joyousness, and a quickening of the moral sense, which is fully as striking and more important both to the individual and to the race than is the enhanced intellectual power. With these come, what may be called a sense of immortality, a conscious-

ness of eternal life, not a conviction that he shall have this, but the consciousness that he has it already.[3]

Prayer and meditation, which focus the concentration, can trigger kundalini. Even when prayer is part of a religious practice, it is leading to experiences, such as the kundalini awakening, that fall outside familiar religious territory. Such experiences should not be denied because they cannot be explained by religious convention. Rather, they should be integrated into the overall spiritual progress. As Greenwell notes:

> The implication is that a number of people in western cultures are finding paths to spiritual awakening not commonly known or supported by western spiritual traditions. It suggests that the rigors of monastic life, celibacy, and disciplined spiritual practices are not essential to awakening, although they may be helpful, and that people living more ordinary lives can have mystical experiences previously ascribed only to saints. It is important to bring this experience into the realm of ordinary life, so that people who aspire to mystic experience will be encouraged to follow this natural impulse of the psyche, instead of believing that only extraordinary and saintly people (so defined by the tenets of some specific church hierarchy) are capable of it. Inevitably, this will bring more genuine spirituality into the culture.[4]

## Diadra

For Diadra, prayer proved to be the gateway to a kundalini awakening, mystical experiences, and an unfoldment of strange and beautiful spiritual experiences that take place in other realms. Diadra is an expert in prayer and has taught the subject to many a theological student. She is a slender, blond woman with radiant eyes that attest to the awe and wonder she experiences. Diadra is not her birth name, but her spiritual name, given to her in her awakening.

"For years and years, my highest prayer has been to know God," Diadra told me. "After exploring every technique I could find for about fifteen to twenty years, I had a mystical experience about two-and-a-half years ago. A few days before the experience happened, I was feeling an intense longing and yearning to know my oneness with the presence of God. I thought I was going to explode if I didn't find this Presence. I went into an all-day prayer vigil with this yearning, burning feeling inside of me. On the second day I had a kundalini experience, or what would be in Christian tradition, the Holy Spirit baptism. A fire started burning in my third eye, and I spontaneously started pranayama breathing [in yoga, a type of breathing through the nostrils that facilitates altered states]. None of this had ever happened to me before. My body started shaking, and I started wailing. The whole thing lasted about thirty to forty minutes. Then I was drawn into a deep state of prayer in which there was communion with the Higher Self. I was told I had just been baptized by the Holy Spirit. Since then I have had an open dialogue with the Higher Self. All I have to do is pivot my mind, and I can feel an energy drawing me in, and there is a communion.

"About a year and a half ago, I was getting ready to go to work, and the inner voice said, 'Don't go to work, stay at home.' I've never missed work before. I missed a week! An energy came over me that literally incapacitated me, it was so forceful. Something opened up inside me, and I received three chapters of a book I was told I would write, titled *The Return of the Dove.* I had been reading *The Keys of Enoch,* but I hadn't been able to understand much of it. I was told which pages to go to so that I could understand what was happening to me. All kinds of experiences happened that week. I felt like I was being infused with this incredible energy. For three nights in a row, I felt like I was being irradiated. The sensation started with my head, and for about thirty minutes the radiation went all the way down my body.

"After a week, the energy left me. I didn't receive any more information until ten months later. Then the last ten chapters of my book came to me through inspiration. The 'voice' identified itself only as the I AM presence, which was giving a message for the book. The I AM is Christed awareness. It doesn't seem to be an entity, like with some people who channel. The I AM told me, 'We don't identify ourselves because there is no individuality. There is only oneness. There is no need for us to be recognized in any way. We speak from the I AM presence.' We are all tied into the I AM, God as I AM.

"What has happened to me since then is strange. I go into meditation and feel this certain energy literally consume me. It puts me into a physical spin. When I'm working with people, I feel this spin, this energy, go out and embrace them. Everybody feels it differently, a feeling or sensation, or a breakthrough. I know it's spiritual energy doing healing work.

"During my private meditation, I've had union. The closest thing I can compare it to is from a book called *I Remember Union,* which is the story of Mary Magdalene and her physical union with Jesus. It feels like every cell of my body is experiencing some mystical union with a high vibration of energy. After that, the I AM energy comes in, bringing in a message from some level of I AM presence that literally speaks through me. I tone and chant, using tones I'm not familiar with. It's as if I am sitting here and yet I have entered into another dimension altogether.

"I get messages from a realm of beings who call themselves the Elders in the Council of Light. They read to me from some sort of Akashic Record or Book of Life, giving me information I am supposed to know, about what I am to do in this life and what is going to happen in the future.

"I can only remain in that energy for a limited period of time. The first time, I became nauseous after about twenty minutes. The Elders said, 'We're going to have to release you now and let you go down to another octave.' I could literally feel the energy release and heat burn off.

"All of this is a beautiful experience, and it makes me feel a part of the cosmic whole. I don't 'see' anything very vividly, but it is though I'm looking through a thin veil between realms, and I can 'see' white-robed beings sitting in a circle. Sometimes there are ceremonial things going on, and they will share with me what that is. It's all very high love energy. Sometimes I think they're coding me, and the codes will be released at a future time when the message is ready to be given.

"Sometimes the energy is so heavy and so strong that it leaves me a little scattered. I am continually being drawn into prayer. It's like I'm bringing down the Christ-consciousness at the soul level and into the flesh, so that the cells are all being effected.

"The Elders have told me that the energy coming into me is to prepare me for work and to be able to stand in the presence of higher angels. They've been taking me at night, showing me signs and symbols. Tongues continue to speak through me.

"I'm learning about other universes, and I am taken places, other planets and palaces that belong to other worlds. Once I was taken into a hall called the Hall of Wisdom, and I was coded with a message that was to be revealed only in a future time. The coding was done by a man in a white robe with a long beard who inserted something into my heart chakra. It was so small, like a little black cube, and I suddenly felt it going into my heart.

"After so many years of prayer and meditation, I have learned how to flatten my mind so that there are no thoughts. When I can stay in that state, the message comes directly through and doesn't register in my conscious mind. The purity of the messages speaks through. I am the spoken word. There is a twin flame being bonded to me that will be the written word. Together we will do spiritual work called Koromanda Om. I don't yet know exactly what all it is, but it is in the process of unfolding, and I am told that it is a mission of love.

"A greater I AM presence is helping me along the way. My belief system has always been that we have a direct communication with God, which I'm finding that this is, but it is different from the way I was brought up. I've had to surrender all my beliefs and preconceptions about what religion is, what God is, and how I'm going to evolve. I feel like a baby."

I asked Diadra how her experiences have changed her spiritual outlook.

"My God has become so overwhelmingly large and yet so overwhelmingly personal," she answered. "What a paradox! All of a sudden I see that God is the creator of all life, and all life extends far beyond what I can imagine—that it is multidimensional, and that we are connected, not just galaxy to galaxy, but in ways that we have no idea of yet. I have a vision of a spider's web that spreads into eternity, in which we are all connected. Each one of us has a destiny within a destiny. We are destined to become Christed beings with a mission and a purpose. We are like flowers in a flower bed, each one a flower but different and beautiful, and contributing to the whole. As we lose our fears and are willing to surrender and trust, then the seals to higher consciousness are broken and the Book of Life can be read to us. We then see and experience what we came to do.

"I teach classes in prayer, and I find more and more people having similar experiences as a result of their opening up through prayer. I'm watching people with gifts and talents just explode with energy. I'm watching the Son rise. It's wonderful and to God it is the glory!

"Prayer opens the mind and heart for the descent of the Holy Spirit fire, or kundalini, which purifies and transmutes into light the accumulated memories of fear and trauma of the past. These are not in alignment with the inner I AM Christ vibration. This is literally the grace of God at work drawing to fruition through the only Begotten, leaving the

Christ in every one of us. We are in the midst of the Second Coming, the birth of Christ Consciousness in all of humanity. We are realizing that our concept of God is much too small. He has created universes within universes, and beings in those universes, and we are all working together to create love and harmony. As we are evolving, we are affecting all these other universes. Billions and billions of light beings are beaming love into this planet to assist in our new birth.

"The Second Coming is an ascension for all of us who choose it. Ascension is going to be a progressive, evolutionary moving into light bodies. We will be able to move in and out of different dimensions, much like Jesus was reported to have done. As Jesus said in John 16:12, 'I have yet many things to say to you, but you cannot bear them now.'

"I do know one simple thing: Love is all there is."

## Prayer, kundalini, and healing

Father John Murray, of New Milford, Connecticut, has had experiences with kundalini, prayer, and healing. Father Murray is steeped in both Western and Eastern spiritual traditions. He was raised in a devout Catholic family, studied in a seminary, and spent a numbers of years as a Benedictine monk. He is a member of the Free Catholic Church International, which has no connection with Rome, and is a psychotherapist. He is a twenty-five-year member and former board member of the Spiritual Frontiers Fellowship International (SFFI) and the Academy of Religion and Psychical Research (ARPR). In addition, Father Murray has studied Eastern meditation and yoga. His immersion in the spiritual world has enabled him to be particularly sensitive to fields of energy, to see and feel energy in ways that many others do not.

Father Murray was in college when he was inspired by new insights on prayer. "The first time I defined prayer, I scared myself," he said.

"I grew up in a very religious, Catholic family that treated prayer very formally. When I was in college and in the seminary, studying psychology and science, I had a great insight: If someone is praying, they're just talking to themselves. They're reprogramming their own computer. I think prayer is a form of triangulation. The triangle is one of the great principles of the universe. With prayer, you create an energy field and reach out to it, and it feeds back to you. That's how you reprogram yourself."

He went on with a laugh, "When I got this insight, my reaction was, 'I've committed a terrible heresy, I mustn't think this way! I must go and confess this!' "

It seems amusing in hindsight, but his reaction points to a pervasive problem: organized religion tends to put prayer in a straitjacket. Whatever religion we join, we are schooled in rigid definitions of prayer. We are taught how to pray. "This way is the only way," we are told. "All other ways are false." We are not encouraged to follow the promptings of our own hearts, the promptings that tell us that there are many paths to God, many paths to the Center, and many ways to pray that will take us there. The heart—the seat of our soul—knows what is right.

Father Murray shared with me two experiences. The first concerned an unusual healing in which the healee knew nothing of the steps taken. The second experience involved Father Murray's introduction to a powerful energy that he would reexperience years later in his own healing.

Back in the 1960s, I went to a Trappist monastery in Spencer, Massachusetts, with a friend on retreat. The Trappists are the most serious contemplative order. Their whole life is devoted to prayer and meditation. My friend bought a little wooden cross in the bookstore as a memento and put it in his pocket. One of the brothers took about six of us on a tour of the monastery. At the end of the tour, my friend asked, "Father, would you mind blessing this cross that I just bought?" The father replied, "All right. Let me see this cross."

He told us all to move back away from him and stand in a semicircle. He took the cross and blessed it in a most unusual way. He held it in his hands and centered himself in a deep, meditative altered state. I recognized it as the raising of kundalini energy, like charging up a battery.

When the father felt he was ready, he raised the cross in his hand and began to bless it in Latin. I suddenly felt this incredible force of energy, like an electrical current, coming right at me. It almost knocked me back. The others felt it too. I could see why he told us to stand back, to minimize the effect of this blast of energy.

Afterward, my friend got an idea what to do with his blessed cross. He lived with his mother. She had been deserted by his father and, as a result, had become an alcoholic and was having quite a problem. My friend had tried to get her to go to Alcoholics Anonymous, but nothing worked. He realized it was hopeless to argue with her. She would go on drinking binges, and he thought he would just have to live with it.

One day he waited until she was out of the house, and he went into her room, crawled under her bed, and tied this cross to the springs under her mattress. Within two to three days, she stopped drinking. Out of nowhere, she just stopped drinking. Then she began to really talk to her son. She knew he was interested in yoga, and she asked if she could go with him to his yoga class. She began practicing yoga and meditation and completely overcame the drinking. She got a job. It was a real healing. He never told her about the cross.

In 1992 I was in Connecticut attending a gathering of the Free Catholic Church International. We are not connected with Rome, and we believe in the absolute equality of everyone, including women as priests. We had planned a big program in which we were ordaining a black priest from New Jersey. He was looking forward to it.

About three days before the service, I was out jogging and slipped and fell and broke my arm right near the shoulder. I thought I would not be able to participate in the service. Someone suggested that I should take part in the healing service done in the evening on campus. The service was conducted by a group of ordained clergy, men and women, who were trained in meditation and healing. There were about six or seven men and about four women. Everyone sat in chairs in a circle, with one chair in the middle. My turn came, and I sat in the chair in the middle. The group began with a meditation. Spontaneously—this had not been planned in advance—the men then all rose and came over to me and laid hands on me. They began to pray healing prayers. I felt the same energy I had once felt with Yogi Muktananda [with whom he had once participated in an intensive week of meditation at Muktananda's ashram], the sieve of fire. I felt a powerful light come down from above and go right through me, down into the floor and then back up, forming a great figure eight, a lemniscate, that went racing through my body. I began to shake all over. It was a high-voltage sensation, like sacred fire ripping through me. It wasn't painful or scary, but I could not stop shaking. I just kept feeling this energy course through me. Then the men stepped aside. I was still shaking.

Then the women came forward and laid hands on me. I felt this huge vertical scissor-like energy, with a zinging sensation. The women began to pray and the energy changed into a horizontal force. Instead of a zing I felt a *shhhhh*. The zing was like sunlight and the *shhhhh* was like the ocean. All the shaking stopped, I calmed down, and the pain left me.

The doctor had given me strong pain pills. I found I no longer needed them. The next day my arm was still sore. But I went to the service, took the arm out of the sling, and participated. There was a little discomfort, like it was wrenched, but not broken.

The day after the service, I went to my doctor to get an X ray. My doctor looked at the X ray and said, "This is very strange." He pointed to the break. "The arm isn't healed, but do you see this ring of calcium forming here? This ring takes at least ten days to form, and the accident only happened to you three days ago. Have you been taking some unusual vitamins or something?" He called in another doctor and they looked at the X ray. My doctor said, "You're very lucky because this is healing very fast." I told him what had happened with the healing service. His only response was, "You know, these things happen. Some people just have a fast metabolism."

I healed up fine in about half the time it normally takes for a break like that to heal.

I think this experience happened to me for a reason. It was a tremendous personal lesson in the importance of energy polarity and the difference between male and female energy. The male energy was like the surgeon and the female energy was like the bandaging. There has to be both types of energy in everything to be healed and to be whole. We must have men and women working together. We must have women priests in the church.

## The new millennium

The emergence of a higher collective consciousness could happen within the framework of Rupert Sheldrake's hypothesis of morphogenetic causation, which was covered in Chapter 2. According to that hypothesis, the fields of behavior established by a critical number of a species in turn influences the behavior of other members of the species—the hundredth monkey idea. If enough of us pray and through prayer open ourselves to spiritual awakenings, then others may be similarly opened through the morphic resonance created by pray-ers.

A similar view has been put forth by the Maharishi Mahesh Yogi, the chief proponent of Transcendental Meditation (TM), a type of meditation in which a person achieves transcendental consciousness by meditating upon a mantra. According to the Maharishi, if a minimum of the square root of one percent of the world's population collectively did TM, the coherence of their brain waves would result in a drop in the incidence of crime, illness, accidents, and aggression. The Maharishi International University attempted to test this hypothesis in 1983 and 1984 by assembling seven thousand persons to meditate. Significant results were claimed, although critics countered that data were selective to support the hypothesis.

Nonetheless, the idea has merit. If a healer can affect the brain waves of a patient, as we saw in Chapter 4, and if group prayer has a greater effect than individual prayer, as we saw in Chapter 7, we have everything to gain by engaging in prayer—and meditation—on a wide scale.

Many persons who have spiritual awakenings or crisis events such as an NDE have visions of a dark future, in which we are beset by catastrophic geophysical changes (or "earth changes") and the disintegration of our society and way of life. Some people take these glimpses into the future literally. While it is possible that such visions represent a version of the future, it is more likely that they are symbolic of the incredible shift in consciousness taking place. Our increasing awareness and accessing of other realities with greater ease symbolizes the "destruction" of our present paradigm, our present worldview. In dream interpretation, cataclysms are often representative of psychic upheaval due to major changes in life. Visions of earth changes should be interpreted in the same way. The old order is being torn down so that the new order, one based on spiritual awareness and values, can become established.

In alchemy one cannot obtain the philosopher's stone to achieve the gold of enlightenment without first going through the darkness, a symbolic death of the old self. Similarly, we must shed the blinders of our narrow approach to God in order to truly see through the eyes of Spirit. We cannot fulfill our potential as *homo noeticus* as long as we hang on to an obsolete worldview. We must be willing to be flexible and adaptable in our concepts of God and our relationship to God through prayer.

This is ultimately why prayer is so vital to us. It is both a catalyst to change and a lifeline through the change. Prayer puts us in tune with the great cosmic flow. Call it God, call it Spirit or Universal Mind, or call it the Tao. When we are in tune with it, great things happen, from little synchronicities, or meaningful coincidences, to miracles.

Humanity has crossed the threshold to higher awareness. How quickly and how well we make the shift depends on each one of us. Experience a miracle. Pray now.

# NOTES

### CHAPTER 2:
### THE ESSENCE OF PRAYER

1. Interview with author, June 1994.
2. Daniel J. Benor, *Healing Research,* Vol. 1 (Deddington, U.K.: Helix Editions, Ltd., 1993), 20.
3. Interview with author, July 1994.
4. Rupert Sheldrake, "Prayer: A Challenge to Science," *Noetic Sciences Review* 30 (1994):6.

### CHAPTER 4:
### PRAYER, PSI, AND HEALING

1. Benor, *Healing Research,* Vol. 1, 107.
2. Interview with author, July 1994.
3. Benor, *Healing Research,* Vol. 1, 12.
4. Peter Tompkins and Christopher Bird, *The Secret Life of Plants* (New York: Harper & Row, 1973), 348.
5. Mochiki Okada, *Johrei: Divine Light of Salvation,* (Kyoto, Japan: The Society of Johrei, 1984), 68–69.
6. Spindrift, Inc., "An Ancient Philosophy, A Modern Test," *The Spindrift Papers,* Vol. 1 1975–1993, B-3.
6. *Ibid.,* G-3, G-4.
7. *Ibid.,* G-4.
8. *Ibid.,* G-4.
9. *Ibid.,* G-4.

### CHAPTER 5:
### PRAYER AND THE POWER OF THOUGHT

1. James Dillet Freeman, *The Story of Unity* (Unity Village, Mo.: Unity Books, 1978; 1987), 47–49.

2. *Ibid.,* 52.

3. Charles Fillmore, *Atom-Smashing Power of Mind* (Unity Village, Mo.: Unity Books, 1949), 133.

4. *Ibid.,* 32, 40.

5. *Ibid.,* 97.

6. *Ibid.,* 72.

7. Ambrose A. Worrall with Olga N. Worrall, *The Gift of Healing* (New York: Harper & Row, 1965), 188–190.

8. *Ibid.,* 190.

9. Mochiki Okada, *Johrei: Divine Light of Salvation,* 83–84.

## CHAPTER 7:
## THE ART OF SUCCESSFUL PRAYER

1. Interview with author, July 1994.

2. Interview with author, August 1994.

3. *Ibid.*

4. Jim Rosemergy, *A Closer Walk with God* (Lee's Summit, Mo.: Inner Journey, n.d.), 50.

5. Interview with author, July 1994.

6. Interview with author, August 1994.

7. Rosemergy, *A Closer Walk with God,* 30.

8. Interview with author, August 1994.

9. Interview with author, July 1994.

10. Dr. William R. Parker and Elaine St. Johns, *Prayer Can Change Your Life* (New York: Simon & Schuster/Cornerstone Library, 1957), 9.

11. *Ibid.,* 43.

12. *Ibid.,* 55.

13. *Ibid.,* 76.

14. Larry Dossey, M.D., *Healing Words* (San Francisco: Harper San Francisco, 1993), 99.

15. Interview with author, August 1994.

16. Interview with author, July 1994.

## CHAPTER 8:
## WHEN IT'S TIME TO SURRENDER

1. Lawrence W. Althouse, *Rediscovering the Gift of Healing,* (York Beach, Me.: Samuel Weiser, 1983), 33–34. First published by Abingdon Press, 1977.

2. *Ibid.*, 56–57.
3. Interview with author, July 1994.
4. Interview with author, July 1994.
5. Althouse, *Rediscovering the Gift of Healing,* 87.
6. *Ibid.*, 88–89.

## Chapter 9:
## "Pure Unconditional Love"

1. Joel Goldsmith, "Prayer," *Science of Mind* 67:6 (1994):7.
2. Judith Green, Ph.D., and Robert Schellenberger, Ph.D., "The Subtle Energy of Love," *Subtle Energies* 4:1 (1993):45.
3. *Ibid.*, 32.

## Chapter 10:
## Prayer, Dreams, and Visions

1. David Engle, *Divine Dreams* (Holmes Beach, Fla.: Christopher Books, 1994), 136.
2. *Ibid.*, 137.
3. Patricia Garfield, *The Healing Power of Dreams* (New York: Simon & Schuster, 1991), 17.

## Chapter 11:
## The Never-Ending Prayers

1. Freeman, *The Story of Unity,* 82.

## Chapter 13:
## Prayer for the Modern Mystic

1. Interview with author, June 1994.
2. Evelyn Underhill, *Mysticism* (New York: New American Library/Meridian, 1955), 306.
3. Worrall, *The Gift of Healing,* 187.

4. Teresa of Avila, *The Life of Saint Teresa of Avila by Herself* (London: Penguin Books, 1957), 42–43.

5. *Ibid.*, 45.

6. Teresa of Avila, *The Interior Castle* (New York: Paulist Press, 1979), 2.

7. Teresa of Avila, *The Life of Saint Teresa of Avila by Herself*, 75.

8. *Ibid.*, 172.

## CHAPTER 14:
### PRAYER POWER FOR THE NEW MILLENNIUM

1. Peter Russell, *The Global Brain* (Los Angeles: J. P. Tarcher, Inc., 1983), 215–16.

2. R. M. Bucke, *Cosmic Consciousness* (New York: E. P. Dutton and Co., 1923), n.p.

3. *Ibid.*, 3.

4. Bonnie Greenwell, *Energies of Transformation: A Guide to the Kundalini Process* (Cupertino, Calif.: Shakti River Press, 1990), 301.

# BIBLIOGRAPHY AND RECOMMENDED READING

Althouse, Lawrence W. *Rediscovering the Gift of Healing.* York Beach, Me.: Samuel Weiser, 1983. First published 1977.

Appleton, George (ed.). *The Oxford Book of Prayer.* Oxford: Oxford University Press, 1985.

Benor, Daniel J. *Healing Research,* Vol. 1. Deddington, U.K.: Helix Editions, Ltd., 1993.

Borysenko, Joan. *Fire in the Soul.* New York: Warner Books, 1993.

Bucke, R. M. *Cosmic Consciousness.* New York: E. P. Dutton and Co., 1923. First published 1901.

Dossey, Larry, M.D. *Healing Words.* San Francisco: Harper San Francisco, 1993.

————. *Recovering the Soul.* New York: Bantam Books, 1989.

Engle, David. *Divine Dreams.* Holmes Beach, Fla.: Christopher Books, 1994.

Fillmore, Charles. *Atom-Smashing Power of Mind.* Unity Village, Mo.: Unity Books, 1949.

Foster, Richard J. *Prayer: Finding the True Heart's Home.* San Francisco: Harper San Francisco, 1992.

Freeman, James Dillet. *The Story of Unity.* Unity Village, Mo.: Unity Books, 1978; 1987.

Garfield, Patricia. *The Healing Power of Dreams.* New York: Simon & Schuster, 1991.

Gawle, Barbara A. *How to Pray.* Englewood Cliffs, N.J.: Prentice-Hall, 1984.

Goldsmith, Joel S. *The Mystical.* New York: Harper & Row, 1971.

Goleman, Daniel. *The Meditative Mind: The Varieties of Meditative Experience.* Los Angeles: J. P. Tarcher, 1988.

Greenwell, Bonnie. *Energies of Transformation: A Guide to the Kundalini Process.* Cupertino, Calif.: Shakti River Press, 1990.

Grosso, Michael. *The Final Choice.* Walpole, N.H.: Stillpoint Publishing, 1985.

Guiley, Rosemary Ellen. *The Encyclopedia of Dream Symbols & Interpretations.* New York: Crossroad, 1992.

Hawkins, Gerald S. *Mindsteps to the Cosmos.* New York: Harper & Row, 1983.

Holmes, Ernest. *The Science of Mind.* New York: G. P. Putnam's Sons, 1938.

James, William. *The Varieties of Religious Experience.* New York: The Modern Library, 1936. First published 1902.

Krishna, Gopi. *Kundalini: The Evolutionary Energy in Man.* Boston: Shambhala, 1985.

LeShan, Lawrence. *The Medium, the Mystic, and the Physicist: Toward a General Theory of the Paranormal.* New York: Viking Press, 1974.

———. *The Science of the Paranormal: The Last Frontier.* Wellingborough, U.K., 1987. First published 1984.

Loehr, Rev. Franklin. *The Power of Prayer on Plants.* New York: Signet Books, 1969.

McLaughlin, Corrine, and Gordon Davidson. *Spiritual Politics.* New York: Ballantine Books, 1994.

*The New Guideposts Treasury of Prayer.* Carmel, N.Y.: Guideposts, 1991.

Parker, Dr. William R., and Elaine St. Johns. *Prayer Can Change Your Life.* New York: Simon & Schuster/Cornerstone Library, 1957.

Peale, Norman Vincent. *The Power of Positive Thinking.* New York: Prentice-Hall, 1952.

Ponder, Catherine. *The Dynamic Laws of Prayer.* Marina del Rey, Calif.: DeVorss, 1987.

Powell, A. E. *The Astral Body.* Wheaton, Ill.: Quest Books, 1974. First published 1927.

Ring, Kenneth. *Heading Toward Omega.* New York: William Morrow, 1984.

———. *The Omega Project.* New York: William Morrow, 1992.

Rosemergy, Jim. *A Closer Walk with God.* Lee's Summit, Mo.: Inner Journey, n.d.

———. *Even Mystics Have Bills to Pay.* Lee's Summit, Mo.: Inner Journey, 1994.

Russell, Peter. *The Global Brain.* Los Angeles: J. P. Tarcher, 1983.

Sannella, Lee. *The Kundalini Experience.* Lower Lake, Calif.: Integral Publishing, 1987.

Sheldrake, Rupert. *A New Science of Life: The Hypothesis of Formative Causation.* London: Blond & Briggs, 1981.

Spindrift, Inc. *The Spindrift Papers,* Vol. 1 1975–1993. Lansdale, Pa.: Spindrift, Inc. 1993.

Teresa of Avila, St. *The Life of Saint Teresa of Avila by Herself.* London: Penguin Books, 1957.

———. *The Interior Castle.* New York: Paulist Press, 1979.

———. *The Way of Perfection.* New York: Doubleday/Image Books, 1964.

Tompkins, Peter, and Christopher Bird. *The Secret Life of Plants.* New York: Harper & Row, 1973.

Underhill, Evelyn. *Mysticism.* New York: New American Library/Meridian Books, 1974. First published 1955.

Worrall, Ambrose A., with Olga N. Worrall. *The Gift of Healing.* New York: Harper & Row, 1965.